A
LINE
IN THE
WORLD

Hirtshals

Lønstrup

Rubjerg Knude

Løkken

Tranum

Bulbjerg

Hanstholm

Klitmøller

Nørre Vorupør

Lodbjerg

Agger

Thyborøn

Harboøre

Fjaltring

Thorsminde

Søndervig

Hvide Sande

Nymindegab

Blåvandshuk

Fanø

Esbjerg

Sønderho

Ribe

Vedersø

Ringkøbing

Skagen

Tversted

Blokhus

D E N M A R K

The Line

It's early summer and far beneath me is a coastline. I have it folded out, a map on my desk. It begins to emerge at the northernmost tip of Jutland in Denmark. Yes, that's where it begins, in the North Sea, on a tapering spit of sandy ground. Then it drops south like a slope. It meanders downwards. Now it has begun, the line. It charts a coast and continues, curving faintly outwards. Then come the cervical vertebrae. They settle one by one, stacked each on top of another, sandy islands. And the line persists, breaking borders, into Germany and on. The islands settle like smaller delicate vertebrae into Holland, now charting not a line but a living being.

A rugged Northern European coastline of roughly 600 miles, from Skagen in Denmark to Den Helder in Holland. From a northern sandy spit wedging itself between Norway and Sweden's unyielding massifs down to the Wadden Sea, where the birds take rest, the hours are counted and the living being whispers.

The line has been a part of me since the beginning. Physically, but on large maps in classrooms too, on television, in the A–Z in my parents' car. Seen in context with

the rest of the country, it looks like the back of a dozy
Jutlander with a silly cap and big nose, facing east. Always
read from top to bottom, from left to right. Never turned
on its head, fragmented, joined or transgressional. On the
map beneath me, the land lies as it lies. A distant coast.
Unfamiliar and raw, considered from a centre of power. At
one time there were scarcely any roads across the broad
heaths of the Jutland peninsula to the shores of the North
Sea, and there were no bridges between Denmark's countless
islands, large and small: the land was matted, impenetrable.
But today the distance between this border and its faraway
metropolises is largely psychological. There are roads into
the system now, bridges over the water, airports and civilized infrastructure. The land coheres, and now it's spread
on the desk beneath me, fixed by a map-maker.

But if I could do what I wanted with time, if I could
accelerate it like a piece of time-lapse footage where the
roses turn from bud to blossom, the line would be alive.
The drawing would always be moving. It would bend forwards, shift backwards, open, turn, perforate; then close,
then open up again. It would vanish in part beneath heavy
masses of ice but be revived as something else, and it would
dance, its tail one moment twisting like an eel, fluttering
the next like a pennant. It is a living coastline made of
sand. Always becoming, always dying. Determined by the
forces of the galaxy streaming through the universe, marked
by the storms, the wandering of the sun and moon, and
human intervention (although the latter is always short-
lived), the coastline has all the time in the world. It is a
long and living tale of tidal waters, subject to the rhythms

of day and night, but, in its reckoning of time, to be considered an eternity.

One line in the world. Just one. It could have been elsewhere and known other experiences, other dramas and silent reflections. What might the line from Utqiaġvik, Alaska to Cabo San Lucas, Mexico have to tell? Myriads. Or the line from Gibraltar to the Cape of Good Hope? There are no borders to the stories told along a line. But a landscape is beyond the telling, like the telling is beyond itself. It takes a person to take up the line somewhere, to open, look and make a cut. This coming year it'll be me, gently guiding the scalpel as I write.

At first I didn't want to. I was supposed to be starting a novel. Then I was approached to write a book about the west coast of Denmark. I said no. They asked me again. And again. I said, 'I'll have to think it over,' and I did. Or I dreamt. In the dream, I was setting off across the landscape in my little Toyota. I saw myself escaping several years of pressure from the media by driving up and down the coast. Me, my notebook and my love of the wild and desolate. I wanted to do the opposite of what was expected of me. It's a recurring pattern in my life. An instinct.

My own geography began in a suburb of Herning, Denmark's answer to Denver, Colorado or Manchester, England. A young, imaginative, knocked-together provincial town in the middle of the Jutish heath. When I was four, my family moved five miles west. My parents bought a tumbledown farm in the large parish of Sinding-Ørre. One half of the parish: green, lush, hilly. The other half: vast stretches of heath and forest beneath a kind of prairie sky, and from the moment I dared to move from place to place of my own accord, I went walking in the landscape. That parish is the only place on Earth where I know all the shortcuts, all the paths, and I know who lived in which house and whose children were whose. I know all the family names on the gravestones. When I come to die, that is where you should bury me.

My family was tied to the place where we lived, but beyond that, we were oriented west. That was where our kin came from; the coastline was our place of origin. My family has had a little house tucked away in a deserted backwater out there all my life. And when on warm days we itched for a quick trip to the beach, we drove plumb west. This was the fastest way to the sea, driving in a straight line until we hit Vedersø Dune. Then we walked across the sand, laden with blankets, thermos flasks and cool boxes.

It was there, one day when I was eleven, that I was nearly dragged out to sea by a wave. I was holding my mother's hand; it was August. In those days I wasn't familiar with the currents, and I didn't appreciate their strength. But as we walked along the beach, letting the waves splash around our ankles, one of them dragged me out. My mother grabbed my leg, and we both skidded on the shingle until it let us go. Afterwards we sat and cried a bit. Grazes on our legs, blood. My mother was clutching my hand and wouldn't let go. Since then I've called them Valkyrie waves, the kind that rove in from the North Sea in long, elegant swells on otherwise mild days. They'll take you to sea if they can. I'm afraid of them, and every time I see them, I remember love.

While my family was oriented in a westerly direction, the rest of Denmark was looking east. That was where the big cities were, and thus the university places. It was the direction you migrated if you wanted to 'amount to anything', as they put it. You had to urbanize, speak proper Danish, live up to your potential over in the east.

It was a shift grounded in the past. In the Middle Ages there was a strong centre of power in Viborg, in central Jutland, but the balance tipped towards Copenhagen, and it's never the losers who get the chance to write history. In the eighteenth century, the golden age of Danish art, painters were exhorted to depict landscapes that defined what the real Denmark looked like. The nation's true nature was to be found around Copenhagen, and it looked like a Hans Christian Andersen fairy tale, a Biedermeier idyll, bare of squalls, wilderness and drifting sands. If the harsh natural world at the periphery was described, it was mostly by the wasteland's priests and parish clerks, who wrote educational tracts about the rows of dunes, about drainage and property rights. Generally viewed from above, looking down. Or with a hunter's gaze, within range and at arm's length.

Women's relationships with the landscape were relatively undocumented. Their feeling for nature was at best irrelevant, at worst dangerous. But now I have claimed the right to see and to describe. The landscape must have an essence that, in itself, can speak. Something that cannot be captured with compasses and spirit levels, that cannot be made harmless with weapons.

I was in contact with this something when I was a child, but like many other bookworms of my generation, I also travelled east. In my first paper at Aarhus University's Department of Scandinavian Studies, I wrote: 'It is in the schism that all identity is formed.' I wrote that sentence in a concrete building in Aarhus, with a view towards the place I came from. A terribly long way from home.

When I think about it now, it feels as though the schism in which all identity is formed made me sew great tacking stitches into the world. I was drawn east, but then back west. I specialized in Swedish language and literature. Looking east, in other words. But it was the Danish and English languages that preoccupied me in everyday life, so west— no, east, zig-zig, zag-zag. I zigzagged until I ended up in Copenhagen, and one day, after several years in the city, I was lying on the floor of my apartment. I had hash dealers below and a young woman who blasted loud music next door. When I pulled back the curtains in the morning, I found myself looking out at a hairdresser's and a block of flats. There was no courtyard to speak of, nothing, only some nearby churchyards and parks. Every day, I tried to find the landscape I missed in one of the metropolis's green spaces, but I was never alone. Never myself. And so I lay there on the floor above the dealers. I'd downloaded an app that played nature sounds from Bornholm, an island in the Baltic Sea. I shut my eyes and listened to the water splashing and chuckling against the cliffs. As far as water noises go, you can't get any further east in this little country. Gulls were screeching softly above the reliable sound of summer rippling. Now and again, if the nightingale wasn't singing, another bird chirruped, a brook tinkled, a cutter sailed pleasantly towards the horizon.

I shut my eyes, as I said, and then it came: I want a storm surge, I thought. I want a north-west wind, fierce and hard. I want trees so battered and beaten they're crawling over the ground. I want beach grass, lyme grass, crowberry stalks and heather that prick my calves until they bleed, and salt crystallizing on my skin. I want vast expanses, wasteland, wind-blasted stone, mountainous dunes and a body language I understand. I want to wake beneath a sky that is grey and miserable, but which creates a space of colossal dimensions in a second, when the light comes ashore. A horizon is what I want, and I want solitude. Healthy solitude, and I want intimacy, true intimacy. I no longer want to be anyone but myself. And then I opened my eyes and took Bornholm out of my ears. My neighbour's everlasting, torturous bass, the smell of hash from downstairs and my romantic let-downs hard-wearing in my mind. But on the back of the living-room door was a map. I'd stuck it up there myself with tape, because you always know before you know—and then I gave up my flat. Three months' notice. I didn't know where I was going, but I wanted to be gone.

Alongside the quiet erosion of my life in Copenhagen, my childhood home in the big, heathy parish was being expropriated. A super-hospital was going to be built in the neighbouring parish, and a motorway laid down. The house was situated squarely on the line that the Roads Authority had drawn to mark an on-ramp. There was nothing to be done. My parents had to pack up forty years and the work of a lifetime and move a mile or so closer to the church. The last time I visited my childhood home was in January 2014. I had just left Copenhagen, my destination as yet unknown. I was living temporarily in a disused school in Dollerup Hills, four hours west of Copenhagen in the middle of Jutland, while my life as a writer had taken an international turn. I was flitting between the USA, the UK and Denmark's outermost province—confounded, bewildered and happy—and now the place where I began was being razed to the ground.

I remember that my parents stood in the hallway when it came time for me to leave. They waited side by side, as they always did when bidding their guests goodbye. The light of the lamp, the same as always. The tiles on the floor, the door handle, the row of pegs. But their faces were going to pieces, and the moment I walked out of the door felt like cutting into flesh. It's possible to have an unconditional relationship with a place. I let the loss consume me all the way to my makeshift lodgings. Then I had to move on; I had to shift the site I came from inside me, turning it into a memory.

One day, having just returned from a trip to New York and Minneapolis, I couldn't stand the uncertainty a minute longer. I bought a house on the central west coast of Denmark. I had wavered long enough. I signed the contract in the pissing rain at an estate agent's office in a rundown rural town. So be it, I thought.

'Let's do this,' I said to myself, and drove off to take an extra look at the house, down a country road with a view over flapping tarps and sopping bales of hay. But far away I could see the sprawling flats and the dunes beyond, a distant and exotic range of mountains. I've always thought they looked like giant lazy camels, with hides of lyme grass and beach grass. A colossal herd of soft and sandy desert animals to be huddled into, sheltering from the wind. Or, on a warm summer's day: to be cuddled, to be loved.

My new house was cheap, practical, and close to the Valkyrie wave that one mild day in 1981 had roved in from the North Sea towards the coast, elegant and combative, to affirm love and drag me with it out into the world. When he showed me the house, the estate agent had stopped at the bottom of the garden and asked me to listen to the rumbling in the distance.

'That's not a motorway,' he said. 'That's the sea.' I expressed the appropriate enthusiasm, but that didn't stop him leaving the 'For Sale' sign in the garage. It would save him the trip, he thought. She won't be staying long, he thought.

But I still live here by the sea. Now and again, when I've climbed the dunes that the locals call 'sea mountains' and I gaze out across the water, the words of the Swedish writer Kerstin Ekman pop into my head. I wrote my dissertation on her, and she has stayed with me throughout my life.

'I have come here often,' she writes. 'A whole childhood, every single day. All these arrivals are false, because in reality I was born here. Here I can do nothing but return.'[1]

But that's just one side of the coin, Kerstin, I think. The other is this: the place you come from is not somewhere you can ever return. It no longer exists, and you have become a stranger. Too urbanized, too acculturated, too loud to assimilate, but all identity is formed in the schism. I will never escape it, and of course I knew that even when I was young. So now I sew my geographical stitches between this coastal world and the savage city. I need the plurality, the conversations, the invisibility and the people. But I cannot cope without the landscape, without nature. I need a broad, still place to which I can return. A horizon. Some friendly, level-headed neighbours. My own place, and a point of departure, where I don't necessarily know all the names on the gravestones, but where I know the light, the scent, the meaning of the shifting winds, and where all the time that's running out is raised up in the telling of a story and snatches its piece of eternity. Before we come apart.

So there it is, the coastline far below me. I'm standing on it in my house on the central west coast, while simultaneously looking down upon it in map form on my desk. I have lifted myself above it for a moment, but for the next year, I will sink myself into it. I shall let it draw me wherever it pleases. I will not let my movements be dictated by the fixed conventions of reading a map: north to south, west to east. I will look at it as a line and dive into it the way one dives into text. It is necessity that will guide me—and seasons, coincidence and memory. I'm not looking for some trumped-up truth about a particular piece of geography. Humans, with our kerosene and our short fuses, have been ranting and raving in nature for far too long. As much as possible, I'd rather be open to the truth that arises between me and the place, at the moment we meet. This is what will happen: I will set off humbly in my restless Toyota. I will find my way with the discarded A–Z that my parents gave me when I told them I was embarking on this project.

'You'll need this,' they said.

All the pages with maps of the North Sea are falling out. They've driven up and down the coast so often in the course of their long lives that the landscape in their book is scarred, furrowed and wrinkled. Coffee stains are legion, and they have entrusted to me a not insignificant legacy. I will grope my way forwards in it. Have faith. I know other people's stories are out there in their thousands, but this is my encounter with the place where the light comes ashore, where the sea meets the beach, whips up, calms, sits up at the table like a creative child, puts greaseproof paper over the map and finds a pencil. The land, now, is engulfed in fog. But I draw a single stroke by following the line I can make out. So there it is, itself, and I shall meet it. See, look—it's moving, the line. It's dancing like a dervish.

The
Shortest
Night

Midsummer. The pace of growth can't keep this up. The corn is turning from green to golden, and everything draws energy from the sun. Today is the longest day. The shortest night lies ahead.

I walked in the heat from the rented cabin on the top of Skallerup Dune, around forty miles south of the northern-most tip of the country, down to the water, amid the scent of rosehips, *Rosa rugosa*, sweetbriar roses, dog roses, roses everywhere. The soil is fat and damp. Yellow water lilies grow in the hollows. Sediment deposited in the Ice Age continues all the way down to the water's edge; the dunes have verdant skin. On the beach, there are preparations for a Midsummer's Eve bonfire. Some children, it must have been, have made a witch with stiff broomstick arms and a wild look in her felt-tip eyes.

It's the time of year when we burn a female doll. It's a tradition, an annual thing in Denmark, an act that has clicked into place. We Danes are more or less in agreement: all of this is a game we play. Burning the evil has its roots in ancient rituals and seventeenth century witches at the stake—we can agree on that too. But it's only in the

past century that the ritual has come into fashion, and
whether it's a cosy custom or a problem is something to
be discussed over strawberries picked for the celebration.
She will be burned. Tonight, as legend tells, she will fly to
Brocken and Hekla: dispatched like sparks above a bonfire, she and her sister witches will celebrate their sabbath
on the mountains there. It's a Midsummer's Eve party: a
celebration of cleansing and the solstice. The light is here,
but the darkness is as well, and now the great wheel turns.
We walk to the holy springs and wash our wounds. Herbs
in the woods and meadows have drunk from the energies
of the universe and drawn rich growth from all existence.
We pick the herbs at night, on our guard against the glow-
worms' bite. We read omens. We tuck flowers under our
pillows. Our brown calves are wet with cuckoo spit, while
the bonfires burn down. It is the longest day, the magic's
night. Everything has opened and yielded. A rattling door
onto the darkness. We burn a female doll in that opening,
and I've never felt much like taking part.

When I was a child, a man caught fire at a Midsummer
celebration my family was attending. It was the host. He'd
built the witch himself the day before, out of a couple of
brooms tied crosswise. He had doused the bonfire liber-
ally with petrol that afternoon, but before the burning, he
thought it could do with one more drop. I saw the thing
myself—him running around in his nylon shirt with a jerrycan, sloshing petrol onto the fire. We saw, too, the lighter,
the spark, the catching, and how someone flung themselves
on top of him to extinguish the flames. They rolled him
around on the ground and crouched beside him on their

haunches as the bonfire burned. It was such a silent, mild night. We could follow the sound of the ambulance all the way from the hospital in the city to far out in the country-side, where we stood, and where the party was over.

It seems impossible to think that this landscape will strike back with savage force in autumn, and that the trees will again be pressed against the earth. That the people now striding straight as rods will need to walk sideways before long. The salt will settle over the beach meadows and on the windows, which will need to be washed again and again. Everything is clear and tender around Midsummer's Eve, and now even here, where nature is harshest, it's soft. Soft and thriftless, I thought, as I stood on the beach and watched a naked Norwegian trying to put on his underpants without falling over. His wife didn't want to come out of the water; his dog had run away. To the south, Rubjerg Knude, a grand ridge of sand; to the north, Hirtshals Lighthouse. Longing for shadow, I went back to the cabin. Then I drove a little way north to Tornby, an area of dunes and scrub and trees, bringing a packed lunch.

Up there the woods were full of honeysuckle, tiny springs with water lilies, ferns, sparrow vetch and wood sorrel. Brown tracks bored into green tunnels. Somewhere among the trees I stood silently for a long time, watching a deer with a fawn. She was grazing, the mother, the little one following. I'm in the way here, I thought, and sat down on a rotten stump with my packed lunch, wood ants scurry-ing beneath me. Above, the intense hum of insects in the treetops. A lone bumblebee that had forgotten it could fly crawled across the forest path. I'm a foreign body, I thought.

I tower above their world. My view from up here is absurd. The only point of me for the forest would be if I dropped dead on the spot and gave the little creatures a good meal.

But this was the longest day, and I walked alive through the woods. I trod carefully. I watched the flowers on the elder trees hover like small helicopters in the dim light, and let myself be drugged by the scent of honeysuckle. Maybe I stole a water lily, maybe a buttercup, and by the time I reached the soft dunes the ragworts were ready, the ticks, the mallow. I took plenty of blood-red cranesbill for myself and crouched by a toad that was resting on a stone. Then home to the cabin on the hillock above Skallerup Dune.

The sun is sinking stoically, now, towards the Norway boat. The ferry, on its way into the harbour in Hirtshals, is balanced heavily on the horizon. They'll be on the deck, watching the coast—the visitors, the homecomers. It's the bonfires they can see, the flames and the lighthouse. There are columns of smoke above the whole country, as though the Danes were busy sending signals, communicating from hilltops, sports fields and allotments. And if anyone aboard a ship in the strait of Skagerrak between Denmark and Norway leans over the gunwale and listens hard, they'll hear folk singing. Yes, in this country we sing in the dusk about peace, 'Sankte Hans, Sankte Hans.' I'm on high ground, listening to the voices rising from the beach. They've lit the bonfire, and the sun has gone nuts too. I hum my own scraps of melody, as the bonfire burns out below. Then a deer crosses the meadow west of the cabin. Then a fox screams. Then the wheel turns, and to the north, the lighthouse blinks at the ferry.

It casts light onto whatever needs to find its way, the lighthouse. I know, because yesterday in broad daylight it shone a light onto me. Hirtshals Lighthouse is white and stately. Beautiful on the soft green cliffs, a fraction north of Skallerup Dune. Everything was infinitely beautiful seen from up there, the green dunes, the turquoise sea. And I could look down on the straight streets of Hirtshals from above. I could see the harbour, where the ferries sail to Norway, Iceland and the Faroe Islands. I could see a camp-site. The weather was fine and I could make out a little group of bathers in the distance. Definitely beach mums, I thought. When I was a child, we usually went swimming on what they called 'housewife beaches', places where the local mothers and grandmothers brought their children because they were safe to swim. The young girls stand at an appropriate distance, clad in new bikinis, gold crosses and their mothers' dialects. A sharp watch is kept on the oldest women. Their skin is tanned leather, their hair clipped short. They have tattoos and big, wrinkled cleavages. They can call a child to their side from the open sea. Now and again, a man in a boiler suit walks past and talks to them. They put up with that, but he can't sit down. They've been skinning fish since before they started school. They've ridden Puch Maxi mopeds, they've gone cruising with drunken men in Ford Taunus cars by the dam. They've cooked more chips than you'll ever eat. They've borne their stormy nights. They have cried when he was at sea, and they've cried when he was home, and they're not for delicate souls. But they are safe swimmers, and if war breaks out, I'd like one of them in my trench. Her and her grandma. They've hauled men's mouths over to the drain in the bathroom. When he couldn't get up, they let him lie. When he wanted to stand, they carried him. Fat, thin, sun-creased, cigarette-smoking, bathing-suit-stretching beauties in the sand. Always swim near them, because the water is theirs.

I explored the view around the lighthouse. Out there was the strait of Skagerrak, turquoise blue and mighty. Around the beacon, bored into damp ice-age cliff: the Tenth Battery. Seventy Regelbau bunkers built by the Germans as part of the Atlantic Wall. Small signs have been affixed to the lighthouse railings, providing distances and directions to various places. From where I stood, it was 82 miles to Kristiansand in Norway. It was hard to get my head around it not being further than that. When I was a child, we often sailed from Hirtshals to Kristiansand in the summer. I thought it took forever. We'd be up at three in the morning to drive north through Jutland. Anticipation in my belly, the duvet on the back seat of the Morris Monaco, my big brothers still asleep and my mum and dad chatting in the front. We were going to cross the sea and drive far up into Norway. On the other side of the water: mountains and eternal snow. It was the late 1970s, and we were going on an adventure. But one time one of my brothers wandered away from the car as we were queueing for the ferry. I remembered that, standing at the top of the lighthouse. He only wanted to get out and take a quick look at the sea, my brother, but what if he didn't make it back to the car in time? What if he was stranded forever in Hirtshals? It made me feel nauseated. I wanted to go looking for him, but at harbours there are quays with edges: they mark the place where solid ground beneath your feet gives way to unfathomable depths. So I couldn't leave the car, and couldn't leave my brother. Such a dilemma, at that harbour: losing either my footing or my brother. But he came back, of course. We sat in the back seat as my dad drove us aboard. All attempts to show how pleased I was to see him were met with an elbow in the ribs.

The power of place. You came here once with all you had, left it and travelled on. And so it is filled with fragments of memory. They flicker, the fragments. They rise like dust in long unaired rooms. In these rooms, I move abruptly, unexpectedly. My movements make the particles rise. They dance in the light, my place-bound memories. Only for a moment, etched briefly in my mind. Most of them never to be grasped again.

So this is what this project will be like, I think, as the silence whistles softly in the lighthouse. Somewhere there's a door leading to an archive of moments that have escaped us. No matter where you linger, you must orient yourself among the records or avoid them, I thought, walking down from the tower.

Sitting with the woman in the lighthouse keeper's cabin, I jotted down in my notebook over a cup of coffee that the Danish part of the coastline has eight big lighthouses. In Danish, this particular type of lighthouse is called an *anduvningsfyr*. The word *anduve*, meaning to approach the coast, comes from the Dutch verb *aandoen*, to sail within sight of shore, to approach from the open sea. These lighthouses are usually tall and powerful, with rotating beacons, and apart from telling people where they are along the line, they guide seafarers into the harbour. 'I'm not scared,' I scribbled.

Now the Norway boat has sighted the beacon, and we light bonfires as we wait for the dark. '*Sankte Hans, Sankte Hans*,' sings the country. Tonight we burn those whose instincts don't conform, but we are civilized now and set fire only to symbols. Cover your child's eyes, for now the flames have caught, and the passengers out on the ferry rest their arms on the railing, looking forward to the holiday or to seeing people back home. They watch the sparks fly, the lighthouse flash. This is the shortest night, and amid the heavy, fertile crops, witches and beach mums creep around in the vegetation. They're gathering herbs for the winter. They're casting runes and searching for signs and counsel in the setting sun. I draw the sun's rays down with me. To travel is to remember. Then the elderflowers light up. Then the fox screams. Then the wheel turns.

Wandering
Houses

It takes a certain build to stay standing on this line. You've got to bend, walk sideways. The old houses have buckled at the knees, but still hold firm. They're digging in to shelter behind the dunes. They shiver on windswept plains behind gust-warped trees. They have hipped roofs and little windows. Everything is about making themselves small, against the pressure of the wind. It produces beautiful houses in concord with the surroundings and themselves. Despite these precautions, many buildings have ended up being blown away, swept over with sand or taken by the sea.

The people who developed the historical building practices along this line knew they weren't living on a western coast. They were living on an eastern one: the eastern coast of the North Sea. If you think of the sea as a delineated geographic shape, then from above the North Sea looks a bit like France. It tapers towards the English Channel, it presses up against Scotland, runs around Norway where the country is heaviest, and down along this eastern coast. The North Sea is a nation without a capital, but with its own powerful identity. At the transition between sea and earth, its vast energy has nowhere to go and surges deep into the land. A piece of the slopes, the dunes, dashes into the sea. Then the fjords break through, then the sea builds tongues, and by the time winter is over the dust-green dunes are as white as Alpine peaks with sand. *Sandknog*, my grandmother called the phenomenon. Sand drifts. She grew up in the early twentieth century in the inland dunes of West Jutland. Sand drifts could eat a farm, a church, a small community, for the wind sweeps in almost every day. It paints the land with sand and salt, insisting that accommodations be made, and there are fierce forces at play. Eager for a closer look, I drove north towards Vendsyssel. I wanted to visit Børglum Abbey and the scenery around it.

It was late June, and the abbey perched on a crest was a safe distance inland. It was the dead calm of summer, and I walked up to the old mill on Miller's Hill to view the landscape and the abbey from a distance. As I stood there, I could—with a little wishful thinking—sense the place where a tiny church had once existed to the north. It had been pulled down before the sea could take it. Now only the bones of the dead occasionally come rattling down the ice-age slope.

I once bumped into a pale tourist by the sea where I live. She was holding a jawbone in her hand.

'What do you do with this sort of thing?' she asked, holding out the jaw to me. I'd been living by the sea for four months. The locals thought of me as a stranger. Strangers thought of me as a local.

I told the tourist that she should call the police. You can't go round picking up body parts without reporting it to someone.

'But is it a dead fisherman?' asked the tourist, and I said it could also be a sailor from the Battle of Jutland, which had claimed well over eight thousand lives.

'And they don't all stay out there, of course,' I added. 'But it could also be from a dead man's mountain.' The tourist was holding the jaw with two fingers. 'I mean, from a mass grave of people who drowned.'

'There are mass graves here?' asked the tourist.

'There are mass graves up and down the whole coast,' I said, 'and the sea eats away at them.'

At that, the tourist handed me the jaw, as though it were my responsibility.

'Call the police,' I said and handed it right back.

From the site up north where the Mårup Church had stood for centuries, and where now only half the churchyard remains, the dead also sift down into the sea at regular intervals and frighten tourists. Sometimes remnants of bone are left devoutly placed on top of the gravestones. Some considerate person disposing of the evidence. You can end up with too many calls to the police when a churchyard is drifting into the sea.

Speaking of the dead, to the north-west I could also spy the colossal dune of Rubjerg Knude. Now that's a sand drift. It has claimed the lives of more than one structure. Not so very long ago the lighthouse that sat atop it was put on roller skates and transported 90 yards further inland. Yes, they put a lighthouse on wheels and moved it, because it was about to drop into the sea. It looks so lonely in its desert, the lighthouse. The sand beneath it has long since eaten up the keeper's cabin, and in ten years, twenty years, who knows, the tower will have to be moved again. It will be impossible to save in the long run, that's just the reality of it; and further south towards Løkken, the remains of summer cabins devoured by the sea poke out of the clay slopes. Septic tanks, drainage pipes, woodsheds—all are wandering down to the sea, accompanied by the Regelbau bunkers. The latter can be found all over the coast, beaten and battered before finally being swallowed by the breakers. The sea picks the meat off them, storm by storm. And there they stay, marked by big Xs so that swimmers don't end up impaled on their rusty skeletons. Once upon a time, they were built to defend a 'Thousand-Year Reich'. The Thousand-Year Reich was afraid its enemies, the Allies, might see the coast for what it was: an eastern shore. As such, it was here that the invasion might take place. Assuming it survived the sandbars. And so the Thousand-Year Reich built a fortress out of concrete. Then it lost on every other front, and the sea has been playing dice with the megalomaniac fragments ever since. Before it swallows them. One by one.

When a landscape is in motion, people and buildings are compelled to follow. This is a basic rule when living with the North Sea. But Børglum Abbey and its willingness to move is a different story altogether, and that was why I sought it out. It sits on a hill by an ancient crossroads, looming unbudgeably above western Vendsyssel. An old centre of power on a fertile settlement. There was a royal estate on Børglum Hill in Viking times, but in the eleventh century the Danes became Christian and the site became a bishop's seat. It was home to the Catholic Premonstratensians and later established as the order's mother house in the north.

As a place name, Børglum first appears in around 1100 as Buhrlanis. The name is made up of two Old Danish words: *burgh* and *lan*. *Burgh* means either *borg* (castle) or *bakke* (hill), while *lan* is the same as the English 'lane'. Børglum, then—a royal estate, an abbey, and now a country house— has been known since time immemorial as 'the castle by the road', or something along those lines.[1] The crossroads is still there. The abbey stands where it has stood for a thousand years. No hurricane can topple it and the sea can't reach it. It has risen above earthly circumstance and will not disappear. Except that, sometimes, it does.

My friend, the author Knud Sørensen, was born in 1928 and has written about Børglum Abbey's peculiar restlessness. Once, in the early 1960s, he and his wife Anne Marie drove down to see the abbey on a clear, moonlit night. They were driving an old Citroën with the children in the back seat, and when they arrived they couldn't find the abbey. They had to drive around searching for it. Knud is a Vendsyssel man by birth. He's been looking at Børglum Abbey since he first opened his eyes. His wife too. They parked the car exactly where they always parked it, and they looked at the place where the abbey was supposed to be. Right there. But, as Knud writes in his memoirs, it wasn't right there:

> We got to the top and we stopped, and we looked around us. Only then did it really dawn on us that we couldn't see a thing. That is, we could see plenty

of things—we could see far across the landscape, and we'd seen the lighthouse at Rubjerg Knude in the north-west as we drove up the hill—not just flashes, but definitely the white tower as well, we recalled. And from this vantage point we could make out what had to be the sea, and we could see for miles over the countryside beneath the bright sky. But we couldn't see Børglum Abbey. Børglum Abbey wasn't there.[2]

I've always found it astonishing that a person so pragmatic, so down-to-earth and fundamentally scientific as Knud could have had a paranormal experience. It also astonishes Knud. Why him, of all people, a man who does not believe in magic realism, who prefers new simplicity? Knud isn't just a poet; he's also a trained surveyor. But perhaps it is surveyors whom Børglum Abbey is eluding, refusing to submit to that sort of profane tomfoolery. The abbey belongs to eternity. 'Measure this, Knud Sørensen,' the abbey thinks, climbing into it for a brief moment: eternity.

But Knud is connected to this landscape, and he knows that identity must be formed in the schism. You carry the place you come from inside you, but you can never go back to it. It's a riddle, but such is life, and Knud set out for Copenhagen as a young man. While studying at the Agricultural Institute, he wrote poems about Vendsyssel in secret. He wrote poems about Børglum Abbey on its hill and Vrejlev Priory a little further inland. He longed to go home to the countryside, the way you might long to see an old member of the family. The landscape made him a poet.

Pragmatism made him a surveyor. Clearly, on that moonlit autumn night, Børglum Abbey was willing to move for both.

As I stood there in the summer's light, the white walls of the abbey were trembling. Flowers trickled up everywhere, but the abbey felt strict and unmoved. It excelled at sober-mindedness, I thought, and its asceticism drew no colour from the worldly extravagance around it. Crossing towards the place where Knud's Citroën had sat idling in the early 1960s, I bought a ticket from a friendly man at the museum shop. I asked him what route I should take around the abbey. He said that if I wanted to learn a bit about the place, there would be plenty to read as I was walking around. I asked where I should go first if I wanted to get the maximum impact quickly.

'The abbey church,' he said.

'Is it open?'

'They can hardly shut it,' he said, and I walked straight over to examine the openness of the church.

I stood quietly inside for ages. I tried to find suitable adjectives, but kept being drawn back to eerie. Was it that the church felt chronically cold, despite the sun in the courtyard outside? Was it the floor's corpse-storing unevenness? The black-painted choir? The heavy velvet curtains flanking the altar? The thought of bishops pushing their baroque bellies through the velvet to make their theatrical entrances? Yes, that's what it was, and it was the cold, and the sepulchre, and it was Christ on the cross with his crazed face, and the armless statue of the Virgin Mary with the Infant Jesus in her lap, his head knocked clean off. More than anything else it was the baptismal chapel: a door, a square room and a font in the middle, crowded round by countless small, malignant-faced boys. Putti, I assumed.

It was as if time did not obey the laws that existed in the courtyard, where visitors sauntered around in sandals to the happy din of the swallows that had just arrived. Yes, it was as though there was slushy snow inside the church. Like it was a winter's day I was visiting, in an age beyond my own, and that only once outside in the courtyard could I pick up my relatively chronological wanderings through life.

Knud is a good friend. I believe him. He doesn't lie, and as I strolled through the landscape amid the chalk-white manifestation of the abbey, I saw it in my mind's eye on a day a few centuries ago. One moment I sensed its age, the next its potent presence. The abbey insisted upon itself so vehemently that it was disconcerting. It played all sorts of psychological instruments to get your attention, and if I'd had Børglum Abbey next to me at dinner I'd have spent most of the time hiding in the loo. In the mild summer weather, I decided to drift towards the café. There, I could get some distance from the atmosphere of the abbey, and I was hungry and thirsty for coffee. I noticed a salmon dish called 'Mrs Rottbøll' on the menu, named after Børglum's current owners. They also had 'Stygge Krumpen' on the menu: three types of cheese, one of them apparently so wicked it could make you cry. Which is fitting, because there was nothing tender-hearted about the last Catholic bishop at Børglum. In fact, Stygge Krumpen had been so vile that people said it was his fault the abbey occasionally vanished into thin air. I heard that from Knud. He got a letter from someone who told him. Stygge Krumpen had been so loathsome when he stalked the halls of the abbey that after he died he burned in hell. As extra punishment, he and his entire abbey were hoisted into the air every now and then for a whizz around the sky. Just so he could see what he was missing. During these heavenly excursions, the abbey was invisible from the ground and it was at one such moment that Knud had visited.[3] Everything had been as clear as an etching in the moonlight—but not Børglum Abbey.

I ate a Mrs Rottbøll for lunch. Precious few people will name a bad dish after themselves. Afterwards, I took a comfortable walk around the abbey, through the herb garden and across the courtyard, avoiding the sucking door of the church. Everything was still. I sat down under a big old oak in a little garden east of the stable block. The tree was stout and inflexible, its branches groping wildly towards the sky. A large privet hawkmoth sat on the trunk, resting during the day. At night it would go fluttering up between the branches.

Time and again, I've questioned Knud about what he thinks happened to the abbey that night with the Citroën. He replies each time that he doesn't know. I've asked him if it might be because places can become so old and full of stories that eventually they start sifting through their memories? That maybe, that moonlit night, Knud and his wife were accidentally caught up in Børglum Abbey's memory of itself when it was still a royal estate? Knud replies he doesn't know. I've asked him if we might be dealing with some sort of time warp? Knud replies that others have suggested that theory to him, but that he doesn't know. I've asked:

'Do you reckon it's a parallel universe?'

'Could the disappearance be a manifestation of the ALL-TIME phenomenon?'

'A magnetic field, a type of cosmic elevator?'

'I don't know, but it sounds brilliant,' is Knud's reply.

To cut a long story short, he doesn't know, and it makes no difference to him. He thinks it works as a story in and of itself. Stories, especially the good ones, are real, and he believes in those. I do too, just as I believe Knud. But I'm not a surveyor. I prefer to take a rather more abstract view of the flowing and cosmic aspects of everything, I thought, and as I sat under the tree I stuck my hand in my pocket. Inside was a lump of amber I'd found by the sea on the way up. I like to put them in my mouth and walk around for a while, holding them there. They feel so warm against the tongue. But the one in my pocket was too big to wander about with it in my jaw. It was milky, round and a little like a child's fist. I looked from the lump to the limed walls of the abbey. They flickered, alive. Nature has all the time in the world, I thought—just look at the amber. It evinces no particular regard for civilization—just look at the septic tanks, the lighthouse. Civilization is a snapshot. Forces such as the sea's, the wind's, the rain's, the ungraspability of the universe, to say nothing of the Earth's glowing core, compared to your reality, strung frail and taut between birth and death? Your concepts of space? The universe would laugh if it knew that you existed and could hear your little joke.

I spent a summer living with an American and his fiancée. It was on the eastern shore of Ringkøbing Fjord on the central coast. The fiancée was a childhood friend of mine, and we took several long walks in the evening. We sat at the end of a jetty and gazed across the fjord towards Holmsland Dune, where Lyngvig Lighthouse flashed. I often sat there alone too, staring at the lighthouse while I thought about where to go. I'd come from New York that summer, and I was moving to Copenhagen in the autumn, but more than that. Where did I come from, and where was I going? I didn't know.

The American told me one night that he often got lost on an ancient heath on the eastern side of the fjord. The landscape shifted beneath him when he walked there. 'Pure and simple,' he said in English. I suggested it was his sense of direction letting him down. He took the insult in his stride. In America there were landscapes so vast that you knew nature had a consciousness all its own. Its sense of time, space, direction is unmoored from our small conceptual world. The locals knew that. They didn't sit on jetties, staring at lighthouses while waiting to move somewhere else. They accepted that it was the lighthouse that could move; or, more precisely, the sandbar beneath it, and that it was merely a question of moving with it. Of being on good terms with the forces of the universe. Having faith that one day you would reach some other place—or home.

The American's story made a kind of sense, I thought. I suggested it to Knud when I questioned him about the vanishing of Børglum Abbey, and he said,

'Brilliant. But I don't know.'

It's a humbling position to be in, I thought, leaning up against an oak tree with the milky amber in my hand: not knowing, not believing oneself big enough to lay bare the riddles of existence. Stick to measuring the landscape as the landscape lies. Don't dream of other dimensions, simply be grateful for the dimension you've been dealt. Maybe it's the Vendsysseler in Knud, I thought, and tilted back my head. I eyed the crooked branches of the oak. How big had it been, I wondered, when Knud was a little boy? Probably more or less a tree already, I guessed. Maybe Knud had passed it as a child or a young man. He could have sat leaning against it, as I did now. He could have looked at the abbey, there as it has always been there. Throughout the lives of his ancestors, of his parents, and his life. As a husband, father and surveyor, he returned one night to find the point of his departure. 'This is where I came from.' And it was gone. One cloudless night he got out of his car and went to meet it. The landscape seemed unreal to him. The colours disappeared, the contrasts grew starker, and Børglum Abbey wasn't there.

Could he see the big oak tree, outlined in the moonlit night?

Or had that vanished too? Still unsprouted, or long since felled?

I looked at the big hawkmoth. Its feelers were like white antlers against the dark bark. Its head was as soft as a cat's. It had been a caterpillar once. Then it transformed, and as I sat there watching the summer tremble, winter cocooned inside it, I knew only one thing: every so often, Børglum Abbey disappears. And some day, when I drive up to see Knud, he'll be gone as well. Yes, some day Knud will vanish, and no one will know where.

The
Secret
Place

There's a place in the meadows by Harboøre, south of the fishing port of Thyborøn. To the west, beyond the slender spit of land, is the North Sea, with its storms and underwater freight trains. Here, on the other side, is the Limfjord, spreading. It's as though it stretches in all directions, taking a run-up before it has to squeeze out through the channel that leads from the fjord to the North Sea. The Limfjord divides Northern Jutland from the rest of the great peninsula, and it's gathering strength before it transforms from fjord to sea. Resting. Nissum Broad, they call that part of the fjord, and on the salt meadows down towards the broad I feel a sense of belonging. I know this marsh like I know my own breath. Same goes for the beach, the dam, the sky and the raised seabed on which I stand. South-east is where the last ice age halted, creating a rampart in the landscape as the ice melted and withdrew. The line that marks the maximum extent, they call it; and I know it.

The Secret Place, my family's little summer cabin, is situated here. Thrust between wild and mild waters, between colossal planes of water, and thus in bold light. From the

kitchen table we have an unobstructed view across to Thy
on the other side of the fjord. We have a similarly unobstructed view of the Cheminova chemical factory. Yes, it
lies across the water, the factory. Has done since the early
1950s, when it was allowed to colonize a bulge on Harboøre
Peninsula called Rønland. In daylight hours it looks like
a rusty red city with far too many chimneys. At night it
shines like Stavanger, in Norway. My dad said so once; well,
actually, it was Stavanger he saw from a mountaintop in the
dusk. 'Hey, that looks like Cheminova,' he said, pointing
at the Norwegian oil mecca, but it's not oil they pour into
drums over on Rønland. It's poison, and for as long as I
can remember we've oriented ourselves here by the direction
of the wind. The wind can be from the north, north-west,
west, south-west, south, south-east, east, north-east—and it
can be from Cheminova. In the 1970s, especially, we had to
drive home to our real house sometimes, far inland, if the
wind blew in from Cheminova. The flounders, which the
grown-ups 'trod' with broomsticks fitted with nails on the
end, had strange wounds, but we ate them anyway. And the
landscape was ours because we were children in it, drawn
in by the smells, the sounds, the shifting light. It was there
that I shaped part of my roots, by letting the iron scent of
groundwater, the marine clay between my fingers and the
salty air seep inside me. Cheminova and its nightlight leak-
ing in—that, too, seemed part of the landscape to the child
that I was. That Folidol, glyphosate and mercury leaked in
too—that we didn't know. My parents believed in the good
in other people. I believed in my parents, and they drove us
home when the wind blew in from Cheminova.

But we might have known better, because there was a man who tried to speak out. His name was Aage Hansen, and he was a not especially tall man in a blue Kansas boiler suit. Blue Kansas boiler suits are called Harboøre suits here, and Aage was a fisherman, so he wore one often. He was also Denmark's first environmental activist, known by the name 'Amber Aage', because he had a small amber grindery at the harbour in Thyborøn. I remember him as a hospitable old man in a fragrant cloud of resin from the grindstone in his workshop. Not a grand man in any sense, but on the wall of the workshop hung a photo of him and Queen Ingrid.

Born in the fishing village of Langerhuse near Harboøre, he knew his coast. Shortly after Cheminova was moved from the area around Copenhagen to Aage's windswept peninsula, so far away from Denmark's centre of power that it might as well be Scotland, Aage started finding dead fish and birds. Realizing what he was seeing, he got upset, got angry, and then he went to war. Not much help was forthcoming from the locals. They'd all got jobs up at the big factory, after all. The silence that can close around someone who says what mustn't be said in a small community isn't for the faint of heart. On top of that, Amber Aage encountered resistance from powerful people, both locally and nationally. But Aage was a fighter, an armchair poet, a fisherman and angry, and so he pressed on. He pressed on until they listened and half-heartedly tried to clean up after themselves. He pressed on, even though they tried to shut him up with the Order of the Dannebrog. Not even when they sent Queen Ingrid up to shake his hand did he stop. He fell silent only when he put on his first pair of slippers, and today his son has taken up the cudgel. There was plenty for the father to clean up, and there is still plenty to clean up for the son. There's plenty to clean up for all of us.

Once a year I walk with someone I care about from Aage's birthplace up along the coast, past Breakwater 42 and onwards towards Thyborøn to eat fish at the harbour. Every year, it's a good day. But it was near Breakwater 42—one of countless breakwaters along this stretch of coastline—that they buried the poison, as though it were an ordinary corpse. Near Breakwater 42, decay smells of chemicals and easy solutions. When I stand there, I stand there to feel it seeping down. It's come to be known as generational pollution, and that's not too small a term. First, the factory was permitted to dump untreated waste water. Then it was permitted to dispose of chemical waste, after which the Danish government stuffed refuse into what's now called the Chemical Depot at Breakwater 42, and then, oops—a storm blew ashore in 1962. It knocked a hole in the outermost dam. The fluid part of the depot drained into the sea: birds died, fish died, and Breakwater 42 was closed.

So they started dumping it on the eastern part of Rønland instead, the tip of the peninsula, which juts out into the Limfjord, and where Cheminova is located. Yes, there. Just across the water from the Secret Place! That's where they buried it instead, and Aage found dead birds, dead fish. He fought. He was encased in silence, just as in 1971 they encased the depot at Breakwater 42 in a layer of asphalt. A little over a ton of sand contaminated with mercury was moved to the sulphur depot on East Rønland. It is there, right there, directly opposite the Secret Place, and while they are burying mercury-contaminated sand, my family is driving up in a black Morris Monaco. My parents are looking for a small holiday home that my dad can use for hunting. Someone mentioned these two acres of land, which extend as far as the fjord and come with a cabin. He turns down the sunken sandy road opposite the church. The car crawls slowly along the track through the meadows, arriving at the spot. An unprepossessing house, around 200 square feet, formerly a barracks for workers who helped build the Atlantic Wall for the Nazis. Latterly moved by truck from Thyborøn further down the peninsula, out onto the fields: unloaded here, where my parents meet it for the first time. The house is protected by a little embankment, and behind that is the privy:

'I can sit down there and watch the birds migrating,' says my dad, and my mum does a complete turn on the spot. It's the horizon she sees. It goes nearly all the way round, broken only by distant church towers. The mucky wall of the line marking maximum extent, the stopping point of the last ice age, to the south-east; Cheminova's chimneys to the north. My mother has smelt the crowberry stalks, the sand, and the salt. It's the potential of the sky she has seen. A place of refuge for the family. The children can play in the sand, she sees. The water in the broad is not deep. The children can swim there.

⚜

It's important to stop by Breakwater 42 every once in a while and remember that, sometimes, people bury enormous quantities of poison in a distant and epic piece of scenery. And the scenery picks itself up, harsh and mild, and it connects. Via currents of wind and sea, migrating animals and people, freight trains and agricultural machinery: landscape has no partitions, not really. What's buried here the sea takes back, and the water bottle clunking among the rocks by the breakwater has been carried here by the currents of the Elbe in Germany, where a person has stood on a bridge and flung it away: *Whatever.*

Easy solutions, long-term problems. The things you'd rather not recall, the things you bury, they take on lives of their own beneath the ground, but truth will out! William Shakespeare knew it, and as for Cheminova, nature itself has played a part in outing the truth.

1976: A storm uncovers the depot at Breakwater 42.

1981: Another hole in the depot: fish die, birds die.

1983: Twenty-one years of dumping on East Rønland stops. Seventy thousand tons of chemical waste are abandoned, with the Limfjord its closest neighbour.

2000: A hole is found in the depot at Breakwater 42.

2015: Cyclones Christian, Xaver and Egon have damaged the depot. It is covered with heavy Norwegian granite.

2018: Sand and yet more sand is pumped around the depot.[1]

We cannot allow any more holes in the depot. A hole is found in the depot. There will be holes found in the depot. There are pesticides in it. Parathion, and there's a hole in it. Before long, there's another one. Storms come ashore. The water rises. The depot is flooded, the depot is eaten away; there's a hole found in it.[2]

But when the lights are on at Cheminova, I don't think
about poison. When darkness falls, the Secret Place on the
salt meadow is transformed into a cave, and those of us
who sleep in it into foxes. We tuck ourselves in, far from
the big city, where a chemical factory might inconvenience
someone. Out of sight, out of mind. Cheminova is feeding
another generation these days, and it still shines industri-
ously at night. I'm an adult now, sitting at the kitchen table
in the cabin. If I set off from home in the morning with a
packed lunch, I can work here all day and feel happily at
home, both in myself and in my writing. A cave, yes, that's
what it is. No electricity, no running water, but I picked up
a jerrycan at Haarum Harbour this morning. The sea pink
whisked back and forth. There was such a light above the
meadows. A bold, deep light, penetrating all that has not
made itself impenetrable.

It's childhood I find here, memories stored. It's my grandmother lying in the hollow of the dunes in her perpetual
synthetic dress. She's got her binoculars; every so often she
dozes off. She's listening to the cuckoo, which she calls *æ
kukmand*. She eats *swotbær*, the dialect word for crowberries.
She teaches me to thread *swotbær* onto ryegrass. We make
bead necklaces out of them, and I say she should be careful
with her nylon stockings, and she says if she ever manages to
stand back up we should go and sit on the knoll. She'll show
me the church towers you can see all around on the horizon.

It's my oldest brother digging up lugworms on the beach;
it's my second-oldest brother flying kites on the outhouse

roof. It's spring outside, but in my memory it's October. We've driven up because it's stormy. We're in the part of the house we call the 'cubby'. I can hear my dad fiddling with his rifle in the dark, but beyond that I can hear the storm. It's an animal flinging itself against the house. It surrounds us. It's a conscious mind that wants something with us, and in a moment my dad will set out into the darkness and inside it. It's 1976, the depot is under threat, and a boy lives a little further down the sunken road. He comes over sometimes and wants to tell me something in West Jutish.

'*We do me mæ nier te a waaaaaa'er,*' he says, and I understand nothing.

'*We do me mæ nier te a waaaaaa'er,*' he repeats, frustrated.

'*Æ waaaaa'er?*' he says, and now it sounds like a question, so I fetch my mother.

'*We hoi mæ nier te æ waaaaaa'er,*' says the boy to my mother, and it's only because he's pointing at the water that it dawns on her what he wants.

But I don't want to go down to the water with someone who speaks a language I don't understand, and it wasn't until I took English in school that I began to understand the language he spoke: *water.* Nor did I realize how deep the roots of English ran until an American told me that 'English came from the Angles, the Saxons and the Jutes'; that wasn't the sort of thing we learnt at school in 1970s Jutland. At school we learnt to assimilate and not stick out like sore thumbs with our halfwit back-of-beyond dialects, but that's another story, because here at the periphery they still speak Scots. Or the Scots speak West Jutish, same thing.

And this was the wildest fringe of the periphery, this place where my parents had bought their holiday home. Sometimes we arrived to find that local biker gangs had shot through the house. For the most part, however, the break-ins took place over winter. The kerosene lamp disappeared, the fishing rods disappeared, my dad's waders, the outboard motor, which was usually kept out of the way in the sideboard, and then the wall lamp that had come with the house. One time there was a lake of piss in the middle of the living room. Right underneath where I sit and write: a lake of piss. Another time, someone had cut themselves in the process of getting in through a smashed window: blood everywhere. And the shovel my mum used to bury the contents of the privy bucket went missing every winter.

Without an outboard motor, you weren't going to get very far on Nissum Broad. Not that you got very far with one either. The water was so shallow that the propeller hit the bottom. Mostly we pulled the rowing boat, a nice one my dad and oldest brother had built together in the grass outside. These days it's rotting north of the house, dried firewood underneath its belly, but one summer in the late 1980s, three of us—a friend, a young man and I—took the rowing boat over to the sandy island that used to be by Cheminova. We pulled the boat out onto Nissum Broad, laden with blankets, beer and packed lunches. He pulled us for a long time. After that, we took turns, because no matter how much we waded and rowed, the sandy island remained just as far away, while the Secret Place receded, smaller and smaller, into the south. Somewhere midway between the house and Cheminova, the water got deeper. My friend was sitting in the boat, while the young man and I trudged inadvertently towards the edge of a dark and slimy world. A tidal drop, an old channel, a dim thicket of seaweed, who knows—but this boundary between the fine, soft sandy bed and the unknown has stuck with me, like a trapdoor in my soul. But we reached the island. A gusty knot by a chemical factory. A single dune swept aloft. Lyme grass and thousands of gulls. None of those gulls were in the mood for visitors. The blanket we spread out on the sand was soon filthy with bird shit, and we fled back to the boat, back across the drop, above the flounders with the strange wounds and all the lugworm castings. They were digging on East Rønland. Shovelling something busily into the ground, but we paid them no mind. We were young, after all. We were going to live forever.

The sandy island is a streak in the water now. Cheminova, across the way, has switched on its lights. I'm writing this in the gloom. In a minute, I'll drive the car into position alongside of the house. Pass the cables through the living-room window, open the bonnet, and then I'll have electric light. They're flashing out there, the new wind turbines in the broad. Sea pink trembles along the path down to the fjord. They're putting in a skate ramp, expanding the harbour, building a water park, and they've got a new ferry in Thyborøn. Modernity has arrived, tourism. The periphery is growing, but down by the harbour in Thyborøn, Amber Aage's watchwords are still clattering in the wind. They're written on driftwood, nailed up outside his amber museum:

My actions will never be governed by the opinions
of others—only by my conscience.

Faith in authority may be wise, but should one
still have faith when that authority is not?

Good question, Aage, and rest in peace. How much of the
salt meadow will be left in a hundred years? More rain will
come, wilder and more frequent storms. This line is made
of sand, quarrelsome but easily consumed. Will the embankment hold? And the inviolable privy, are its days numbered?
We flew kites on its roof. We tied strings to plastic bags from
the supermarket and watched them flutter in the wind. We
played games, tossing a ball back and forth over the low
house. I don't belong here, according to the locals, but I have
roots here. Strong roots. They run through my senses, my
family, our history, and they reach my love of the Limfjord
and the North Sea. They run down through the sand, the
marine clay, to the groundwater and the ochre. They run
down into the depot. The storms are coming. The water
level rises. There will be a hole in the depot.

West
by Water

I've always felt a bit sorry for people who are landlocked. And if on top of that you're feeling stifled by the government, then no one can blame you for upping sticks and moving to the water when you see your chance. People gather up their petty things, travel, and here she stood with salt in her hair. I was given leaflets—she had plenty of time—and she led me into a special room in the keeper's cottage. It was full of windmills. Windmills made of Lego, windmills made of wood, windmills as tall as a person. On one of the biggest windmills in the room, a father or mother had, at the urging of a child, put a little Christmas tree on top.

If there were windmills in the keeper's cottage, it was because they were outside too. I could see them from the top of the lighthouse. From the beach, strange churning breakers were moving out to sea. This was Horns Reef, and I followed it with my eyes. Somewhere that seemed infinitely far out, I saw them turning: the turbines of an offshore wind farm known as Horns Reef 1. Looking closer, I could pick out the blades of Horns Reef 2, turning in a distant light further on; and perhaps it was my imagination, or maybe the turbines' absurd height, but I thought I glimpsed the colossal shapes of Horns Reef 3. Those are the ones furthest away, and if you count the blades, they're nearly 600 feet tall. They bore 130 feet down into the sea. Each blade weighs 33 tons, but that's nothing compared to the 381-ton towers. They are the windmill's answer to giants, and they loom tall between 18 and 27 miles out, white trees with circular branches. Their roots are a network of cables that burrow down beneath the seabed to a transformer platform, and the transformer platform's network of roots are submarine cables that conduct electricity to the coast, where they merge with an onshore cable that wends its way inland to the high-voltage network, bringing roughly 775,000 households all the electricity they could wish for. I read all that in the leaflet, but struggled to get my head around it. The white forest out there had been built by humans wanting to colonize the world with a green future. Yggdrasil in plural.

I gazed for a while towards the Skallingen Peninsula in the south. Until well into my lifetime, there were Second World War landmines buried out there. You could go for a walk and get your legs blown off by the past. The bunkers are still there, but some of them have been remade into sculptures. They've had donkeys' tails and heads added, with the German concrete forming the body. They look like some kind of sea creature: half horse, half fish. Their muzzles are aimed at England, and they were made for the fiftieth anniversary of the liberation. They are mules, meant to symbolize peace because mules cannot reproduce.[1] Rather an unpleasant metaphor, I thought, walking around the lighthouse beacons, peering north across Kallesmærsk Heath. The heath is a military training area that extends quite far north. My dad told me about it over and over, talking about his time as a recruit at the barracks in Varde. About training exercises on the heath and in nearby Oksbøl. About aiming for Mosevrå Church when adjusting your howitzer. It was a small, modest red-brick church with a tiny spire on the roof like a growth—eminently suitable for target practice. He told me, too, how he and my mother had met at a demob ball in Varde.

'I hit a bullseye there,' he likes to say, because she wore
pirate-style trousers, had fiery red hair and was a warrior
in her own right. And so the landscape here represents a
fateful moment in my life. A chance encounter, that's me;
and here I was standing at the top of the lighthouse, gazing
down on my haphazard start. They still play war games on
the heath. Maybe they still point their guns at the church.
And the German bunkers are among the breakers, turned
to mules now, in what looks like a wild ride west. Mules
riding Englandwards, tails whipping and muzzles frothing.

Once upon a time there were Viking ships in those breakers, their bows fixed in a westerly direction. Now those were
warriors. They sailed for England, Scotland, Ireland and the
world in general. They had wonderful ships, the Vikings,
and weapons on board. They mastered the sea, read its laws
and learnt them by heart. At night they navigated by the
stars and a frantic desire. Thus coastlines were decoded,
the mouths of rivers overcome, and the ships shot fast as
darts. The keels were made of huge single pieces of oak,
so that the great breakers out at sea could be brought to
heel. The ships rode high enough that they could travel up
a river, and the mast could be taken down. It was possible,
this way, to creep up on the blameless monks and villagers
in far-flung lands, or indeed anyone else they considered
prey. Shield and sword. Mines and howitzers. My mother
in pirate-style trousers.

In her book about the Vikings, the archaeologist Jeanette
Varberg writes that the fleets set sail from West Jutland
and the Limfjord, among other places. Depending on the
weather, it took them three days to reach England. Three

70

days in a wooden boat, with a sail to harness the wind and
men to row. Stinking, pissing, lice-ridden warriors aboard
with nothing to lose: sea stallions. In my day, the ferry sailed
from Esbjerg to Harwich in around nineteen hours, and
you could buy cheese toasties and dance underneath a big
disco ball as you crossed. We had sea stallions on board too,
but they wore tennis socks and sneakers. I miss that ferry,
and the bland taste of Pisang Ambon liqueur. The crackly
loudspeakers, the deep rumbling heartbeat of the vessel,
and the cabins reeking of sleep. I miss the slowed speed,
the patience, the 'let's just take our sweet time reaching
the coast of Great Britain'. We've done it before, and we
can do it again. The entertainment awaiting us isn't going
anywhere. So we sail in reverent silence past the white, wind-
turned forest. Spare a thought for Odin, who hung from
Yggdrasil for nine days and nine nights. Let the ravens fly,
the horizon draw us on: the British Isles have come to stay.

We've sailed this route since time immemorial. Long
ago, the Angles, who lived on the part of the North Sea
coast we now call Schleswig-Holstein, and the Jutes, who
roamed further north, crossed over there together. They
were migrants, of a kind. Now and again they brought
the Saxons too. The seaborne trio: the Angles, the Saxons
and the Jutes. They made black pots, sang songs and had
children with the locals. The English soil was like the soil at
home, and so the exports of the North Sea coast consisted
not merely of death and furore: later there came oxen too.
They drove their livestock along the Ox Road, down through
Jutland into Schleswig-Holstein, Friesland and Holland,
then sailed them to England. Such is the way of trading

warriors. First black pots and livestock. Then bacon, porn and Lurpak—but that came later, much later.

Fast-forward through the Viking era, to its glory days: sources, archaeological finds and the increasing number of Danish words in the English language suggest that at least 30,000 Scandinavians settled in England towards the end of the ninth century. The Danelaw, the area of eastern England where the Scandinavians—after endless battles with local chieftains—set up a parallel society with its own laws, had a profound influence on the English language. More than six hundred words have been adopted from Danish: sky, cake, law—and water, or *waaaaaa'er*, in my personal opinion.[2]

The route west across the water, dangerous and exciting, charged with violence and the thrill of the foreign. It's customary to date the beginning of the Viking age to the 8th of June 793 exactly. This was the day the Vikings landed on Holy Island off England's north-eastern coast. Situated on it was the priory of Lindisfarne. Isolated, simmering in quiet contemplation, its cellars stacked with gold. The Vikings took what they wanted when they arrived. The reason we're able to date their arrival on Lindisfarne so precisely is that the monks at the priory had learnt to write. They diligently recorded the violence that had come upon them, worrying meanwhile about the poor heathens' souls. Their hands were a jumble of rosaries and defensive wounds, and they wrote how surprised they were that it was possible to travel so far by sea.

But travelling so far by sea was indeed possible, and had been for a long time. In every direction, in through the Baltic and up through Russian rivers. Down along the

European coast to the Middle East, to Africa. Across the Atlantic to a place they called Vinland, which would later become America; they set foot on Greenland too, and they sailed into the heart of Europe, setting fires, trading, whoring. Nothing to lose, and home they came with treasures, people they'd enslaved, and distant ways and customs. They ruled over England, and their actions left traces across wide regions of the world. The Arab writer Al-Mas'udi described these fire-raising heathens in the 890s:

> In the extreme North [...] where the influence of the sun does no more than alleviate, and the regions have more than their share of cold, damp and snow, the people are characterized by a good physique, ill-bred behaviour, slow speech, sharp tongues, fair skin, powerful flesh, blue eyes, curly and red hair. All these traits are due to their damp countries, and their cold nature is not conducive to strong religious faith.[3]

One senses that Al-Mas'udi thought of these Northmen as a people sprung from the edge of the world, but that wasn't how the Vikings saw themselves. They didn't feel as though they lived on the fringes of anywhere. They had long ago become skilled at operating over much greater distances than most. They knew that there was land on the other side of the great sea. They knew, too, that it was easier to cross long distances if you went by water. Travelling by land was slow, but the sea—ha! And new worlds were hiding in the waters. On the other side of Horns Reef, for example. They knew there was a country beyond, and they knew they could reach it. In his book *The Edge of the World*, the English author Michael Pye suggests that they most likely navigated not simply by the stars but by the wide-flung horizons. It had taught them that the Earth was round. They knew they could sail so far out to sea that the Earth itself would conceal them from the land. 'They used every advantage that a round Earth could provide,' writes Pye.[4] And this is one of the most inspiring things about the Vikings: they had grasped that the Earth was round, and if the Earth is round, then you can't live on the edge. No matter where you are, you're always in the centre. Confident in this knowledge, they cast out west by water to expand their territory and live their short lives while they had them.

It's a fantastic story. Complex, wide-ranging and steeped in the atmosphere of the sagas. Incomprehensible in its daring, its beauty and its cruelty, and for those who crave raw masculine strength, who yearn for blood and honour, it's easy to tap into. It can lead them down all sorts of wrong tracks, until sometimes they end up as bunkers on the beach by Blåvandshuk. As mules of peace with Nazi bodies. Tough to shake off. Like my mother with her fiery red hair at the demob party—that image, too, is tough to shake off. She rode a scooter and backcombed her hair. At school, she was teased for its coppery redness, but she dreamt that it was passed down from an ancestor who had sailed the seven seas. When my dad introduced her to his parents, my grandmother said, 'We'll never get that hair out of the family now,' and so it was: my mother passed her red hair on to me. We have Celtic blood in our veins. That red hair came to Jutland from the British Isles, after all. I was thinking about that as I stood in master carpenter Skafte's lighthouse on Blåvandshuk, surveying the wind-propelled giants. How the mind-bending coincidences that went into me were all of a piece with what was over there—bound by family ties that run so far back in time you need your imagination to help you understand it.

When does a story begin? Always somewhere else, always further back in the text, beyond the horizon, in the unknown, under Yggdrasil, perhaps? Or a gigantic wind-fed tree contrived by engineers. It's hard to say because the past's unfolding is double-edged. Everything changes, but the essence remains largely the same. The Jutish west coast, which I saw from the top of the lighthouse, has undergone major changes, yet it's still the same. In Viking times, the water's edge was much further out than it is today. The sea gnaws, taking not just land but archaeological finds that might tell us who we were, where we came from, and with whom we fused out at sea. Ribe, south-east of Blåvand, is Denmark's oldest town. In the Viking era, it was a long journey from its closest neighbour, Dorestad in Friesland. We know that. And yet we don't, because there might be a town in the North Sea that we've never seen. An Atlantis full of purloined reliquaries and gold from Lindisfarne, Arab silver dirhams, small ritual statuettes sailed in from the cradle of humanity, amber beads, glass beads, golden treasures and seeresses' staffs. Somewhere out there may be an underwater town of slaughtered horses and decapitated slaves, buried in stately ships with a lord or a lady whose name has been devoured by time. Yes, out there in that

North Sea Atlantis are royal estates and ring fortresses, rearing bowsprits, the carved heads of dragons and splintered shields. Out there, the age of the Vikings has gone down to rest on the seabed, among the seaweed and the shoals of herring. The passing sun plays through the water on all the things we have forgotten, or never came to know. The past plays out in depths haunted by shadows.

But out on Horns Reef, new warriors are at work. The giants are turning, dreaming of a fossil-free future. Our new warriors—engineers, operators, service technicians—set out into the world and build forests of wind. It's Vattenfall, not Valhalla, they've got in mind. They build roots from electric cables; they are climate-smart. It's hard for the eye not to rest on the turbines. Standing in the lighthouse, it felt as though I longed to join them. There, at Denmark's most truly western point, something important was beginning. Maybe one could sail out there and circle the trunks. Maybe one could reach them in a helicopter. Fly in and out among these trees of the sea. Watch the wind pluck at their flawless branches. Find one's origin, or finally escape it. I longed to be in the nacelle during a raging storm. To be drawn into its power, enveloped by it, lifted, carried, shattered. To be a Viking or a small animal in the North Sea between Blåvand and Harwich. To live my brief and arbitrary life while I still have it.

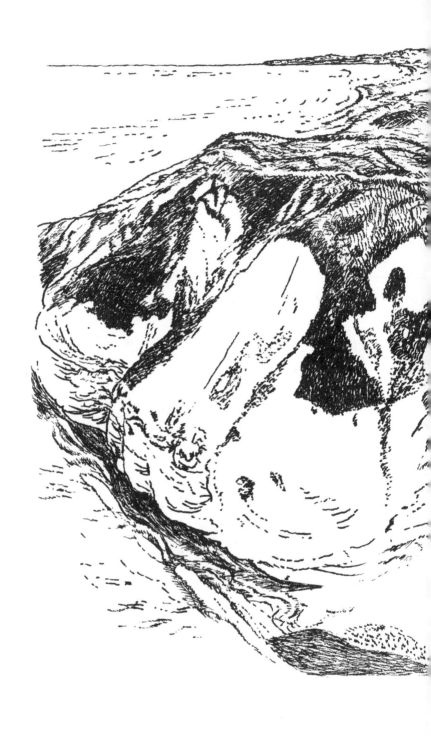

The Tracks
around Bulbjerg

I't's exposed as a stump of tooth. Snapped at the root, where the nerves are laid bare. It should have been bristling with birds out there, potent, a landmark above a Jutland where nothing is as hard as rock. Except right here, where the bryozoan limestone has erupted into bird cliff. To the right of where I stand is Bulbjerg, the Shoulder of Jutland, towering 150 feet above me. White, hard and mighty, in a cloud of kittiwakes. A bulwark.

Below the kittiwakes is another bulwark. This one consists of bird photographers. They have Saturday meet-ups, and they have camouflaged lenses. Some wear clothes that help them blend into the vegetation. They have one foot resting on a piece of limestone, their telephoto lenses collectively erect, all the better to lean under Bulbjerg with. They aren't rare, the kittiwakes, but they're rare in Denmark. The photographers follow them doggedly. I wonder what they think, the birds, about the other flocking species down below. They seem indifferent, but maybe, if you got close enough, you'd see in the kittiwakes' eyes that they miss the proud column of rock that once jutted out of the sea: Skarre Cliff.

It was shaped like the bragging bow of a ship, and the Vikings must have seen it as a sign. For thousands of years, it held its head high. Now it's just a little stump of limestone in the sea, gnawed down. But before it fell, it adorned postcards and stamps. It was a mystery and a place for day trippers. It gave west-coast Jutlanders faith that the sea did not take everything. Something, no matter what, was still standing. And then, one night in 1978, my dad pauses in front of the television. It's the news he's watching, and strictly speaking I'm supposed to be in bed. But something has happened. They're talking about the storm sweeping across Denmark. They're showing pictures of Skarre Cliff, and then they cut to an empty sea. Where Skarre Cliff had stood, now there is nothing.

My dad grew up in flat, potato-growing country. That's why we go to Norway in the summer: we go to see the massifs. We go to experience what it's like to stand somewhere high up in the landscape and look down on it at the same time. When it comes to mountains, Jutland doesn't have much to offer. That's what my dad says, looking down his nose at Sky Hill, the highest point in Denmark. That heap of earth. But Skarre Cliff and Bulbjerg stand firm. We've been on excursions out there, and they're not going anywhere.

And then Skarre Cliff did, after all. It's like the sea gently pushed it off its pedestal overnight.

My dad doesn't say anything, but I can see him crumbling in front of the television. Now my mum's there too. Her arm around my dad. He's crying because Skarre Cliff has fallen. And he's crying because his big brother, my uncle Erling, died in a car accident not so long ago. I'm in my pyjamas, and I feel grief spawn. A loss is final, I understand in my nightie, and the losses are piling up around Skarre Cliff.

But the kittiwakes fly. No matter what. They simply transferred from the snapped-off bird cliff to Bulbjerg itself. That's their nature: they let time pass through them, egg by egg. It's summer now, roughly forty years later. Lyme grass whispers behind me. Uncle Erling is still dead, and Skarre Cliff will never rise out of the bay again. But the rest of us are still here.

'Gripping!' scream the kittiwakes. 'Gripping!', and I straighten up. I want to head round to the other side of Bulbjerg, where you're backlit at this time of day. The back-lighting reduces the kittiwakes to meaningless shadows, so the photographers prefer not to stand around there. Bulbjerg protrudes over the sea, white and dripping. Along the beach are smooth-honed limestone cliffs. They look like the bones of a giant. Now I'm standing on a shoulder blade. Now I'm stepping over a pelvis. Then I'm walking down a sandy track away from the beach, up towards the great skull of Bulbjerg, chalk-white and covered in low vegetation.

⚜

There are paths all over the place around here. They criss-cross up and over the big chalk skull like sutures. They branch off, drawn by living feet, in and out of the under-growth. They find their way.

'The track begins where the grass has bent. Summer after summer. Under soles and hooves and weight, the action is repeated, until at last the blueberry stalks come to know it and to bend,' writes Kerstin Ekman. 'A network of paths, veins, vessels of memory...'[1]

I once learnt that quotation by heart. It combined two of my passions: literature and paths. For at the end of the path, there was always something hiding. The path went there for a reason. Someone wanted something there, and their wanting was an etching. Sometimes it was a little house, a fjord, a flowering tree or a sea hidden at the end of the track. Other times it petered into nothing, but nothing was also something. You could stand and look. Or sit down, reflect or carry yourself to some new place. I have a fondness for the routes few people take, but here at Bulbjerg the paths are well trodden. Tourists scurry over the limestone like perpetually hoarding mice.

My feet choose a path on the south side of the cliff. I clamber upwards. When I turn around and look down, I see other paths trickling into the countryside. Maybe they were first used by a marten, then by a fox, then a deer, then a badger, then a person, then another person, until at last they were bit deeply into the landscape. There are paths everywhere, up and down the coastline. A path is drawn in the sand, perhaps, and then a storm wipes it away, so the feet find another. Maybe the track is used mainly for practical purposes, and so it's paved. Then come the bicycles, the buggies, civilization; and civilization shores up the stories it tells about itself, while these feet-laid paths shift easily from year to year, until perhaps one day they're gone. One of my most secret paths along the coast is the one that led down towards the east side of Ringkøbing Fjord, hit the beach, and continued out onto a rickety jetty with a clear view over the lighthouse on the other side of the water. The lighthouse was flashing, unbreakable in my memory, with all its questions about direction in life. Another path I love is the one that goes from our little summer cabin, the Secret Place, onto the amber beach, past the old tar barrel, and finally down into the water, where Oddesund Bridge quivers like a mirage in the distance. At the end of that track are geese, golden plover, curlews. There is amber in the east wind, and the memory of bonfires with those I love, that's out there too. Yes, I prefer living tracks, ones that talk to the landscape this way. 'Vessels of memory,' as Kerstin Ekman writes. 'To be led along. To move with the slowly pulsing water and yet be still. Like the plants in the brook, like the hornwort and the water lobelia.'[2]

This eternal, fertile and dread-laden stream inside us. This fundamental question: do you want to remember or forget? Either way, something will grow. A path, a scar in the mind, a sorrow that you cannot grasp, because it belongs to someone else. All that must be carried alone. All that cannot be told. Your story emerges in flashes, or as ripples on the surface, before diving down again. Your memories want you and do not want you. Your story is the one you share with others and the one you must live with, in yourself, and no matter what, you are led along. You are moved, transported, forced to wander down all these tracks, into the light, into the dark, into nothing.

Once, at a book fair, I met the Norwegian author and neuropsychologist Ylva Østby. Her job is to understand these vessels of memory. She gave me one of her books. I don't have it with me at Bulbjerg, and right now it would be great to ask Ylva. And, indeed, I can ask Ylva, always. She told me so. Now, standing on a path on Bulbjerg, I message her.

'Hi Ylva, I'm standing on the only thing in Jutland that's remotely like a mountain. There are loads of paths round here. Would you say that paths and memories are similar?'

Ylva lives on the other side of the strait and works at the University of Oslo. She's often online, so it's worth taking the chance. I sit down on a tuft of heather and gaze out at the stump of tooth. The water is lit by a glimmer from below, like chalky light. Before long, I can see Ylva is typing.

'Sounds like you're somewhere beautiful,' she writes.

'Not exactly the Trolltinden Mountains,' I reply, 'but it doesn't get any bigger here. Am I on the wrong track?'

Ylva thinks in Norway.

'When a memory pathway arises in the brain,' she writes, 'it can be similar to the way a path forms over time: two neurons keep stimulating one another, and gradually a stronger connection develops between them.'

I'm not used to neurons, but I respect them, and I can see that Ylva is elaborating.

'Plus our surroundings help us to remember,' she writes.

'Our surroundings?' I ask.

'Yeah,' says Ylva. 'The paths through the landscape are a feat of memory that we create with the landscape and with the other people who have walked and are walking through it.'

A kittiwake flits past above me, then another. The bay is a cone of blue.

'Many paths are thousands of years old,' says Ylva. 'They knit places together in a way that worked well for the people who lived before us. They work well for us too, so we don't have to find the same paths again.'

That's civilization for you, I think. A track becomes a path, the path becomes an old road, becomes a country road, becomes a main road, becomes a motorway; but once it's become a motorway it has long since stopped talking to the landscape, I know. Ylva continues:

'The landscape still bears traces of individual human beings' experience of it.'

That's infinitely beautiful, I think, and Ylva writes:

'Your memories of a particular landscape are stored in a network connected to all the associations you had when you went there for the very first time. When you go back, it activates that.'

The edges of the harbour quay, the presence of death, I think, and write:

'The landscape is an archive of memory.'

She answers with a smiley and points out that nature also permits certain culturally determined associations. It's important to remember that.

'For instance, I see trolls when I go down to the woods,' she writes.

'You see trolls, Ylva?'

'I do, yes,' she replies. 'The trolls are something the forest lets me see, but the fact that I see them is also due to the cultural heritage I bring with me into the forest.'

I ask Ylva if that's why I've never seen a troll in Norway, even though I've been there a lot. 'I mean, is it because Danes don't bring trolls with them—they're not part of our cultural associations? Unless you're from Bornholm, I guess.'

Ylva confirms this, and I decide to end the conversation by boasting that I once saw an elk in Norway. After that, Ylva has to go. I thank her for her time, and then I'm alone on Bulbjerg once more. Ylva is embedded here now. I can never cross Bulbjerg again without thinking of Ylva Østby.

⚜

I sit there for a while, taking it in. Thousands of other people's memories coexist here: memories of a summer's day, of a stinging jellyfish, of a storm. Memories of blind man's bluff. Memories of violence. Of people who came and went, of houses that once stood but stand no longer. People on foot, people on horseback, and now the sky is high with summer. Behind me is the green countryside: hills, cliffs, trees and paths, meeting and diverging. They must look like nerve cells from above, and once upon a time, there was a seaside hotel on the top of Bulbjerg. I believe it was the Germans who pulled it down. They were afraid such a big white thing would attract Allied bombs. So they burrowed down into the skull instead.

I try to imagine the time before the war. I use my collective culturally determined memory to access the associations: over there is the hotel. It looks like a castle with its tower. The upper middle classes stroll around in white dresses and summer suits. I see straw hats. I see privilege. I see lolling guts, and I see the author Thit Jensen. Yes, Thit Jensen. Small and plump, she traipses back and forth in flowing clothes. Her husband is busy painting the hotel dining room with local motifs. Meanwhile, she wanders, drawing inspiration. She has no children, and is notorious in the press for this and that. Partly it's this dereliction of her duty to reproduce; partly it's that her husband is eleven years younger than her. She makes no bones about being an advocate for abortion, women's liberation and other dangerous things. She is the sister of Johannes V. Jensen, winner of the Nobel Prize for Literature, whom everybody is obliged to love and honour. But brother and sister do not get along. He is fascinated by machines, she by women's rights. The sibling bond breaks, and no, Thit has no children, but she is a spiritualist, so she has the dead, and she's especially enthralled by the area on the other side of Bulbjerg. It's called Dead Man's Flat, and if she's drawn to the place, it's because she has met a spectre there. She communicates with the ghost, and that, too, is a feat of memory. While her husband is painting at the Seaside Hotel (or while he's screwing her best friend), she goes to speak to the dead man on his flat. It's a sailor of the world who's buried there, most likely. She imagines a member of the British aristocracy. Noble, with a dog, possibly a greyhound. But he can't find peace, and nor can she. She talks about that to the dead man, the restlessness. He doesn't answer, but he hears her out. The spirit of the greyhound roams across the flats, and she goes back to the hotel and wishes the living dead. I imagine this, just as I imagine that precisely where I'm standing now, on top of Bulbjerg, is where the idea came to her for her novel *The Erotic Hamster*. *The Erotic Hamster* is embedded in the

The Timeless

W e've been planning this for years, and now we're
doing it. We could easily spend a long weekend; now we're
doing it in one day. We've chosen the stretch of coastline between Ringkøbing Fjord and the Limfjord. Midway
between these two points is my home, and I picked up Signe
at the station last night. That was Saturday. Today we're
feinting our way past the services and into four churches.
I've been in touch with priests, church wardens and sextons.
Everything is arranged. We've got coffee in a thermos. Signe
has brought her sketchbook. I have brought my Moleskine.
It's mid-August. Last night a heavy rain washed in from
the sea, dragging a gale. Today the sun is shining, but
there's a strong wind. It tugs at my little Toyota as we
drive south to our first stop. Just beyond the dunes, which
in this scene are to our right, the sea is whipping a brisk
gale into a stormy one. This will be a two-hands-on-the-
wheel sort of day.

My friend Signe Parkins is a draughtswoman and visual
artist. We both love frescoes, so now we're using one day,
one sketchbook, one Moleskine and one Toyota to explore
some of the frescoes along the central west coast. We can

manage four churches out of the many churches there are—
and there are a lot of churches in Denmark. The Norwegian
writer and poet Bjørnstjerne Bjørnson, after clambering
up to high ground on the island of Mors in the Limfjord,
supposedly once said that with the number of church towers
he could count from there, the locals were either very godly
or ungodly lazy.[1]

The first churches were made of wood: stave churches.
Then a travertine church, apparently English-built, appeared
in Roskilde about a thousand years ago. Next, to the north,
came the German stonemasons. They were meant to teach
the Danes to build with stone, and they did. In a few hundred years there was scarcely a knot of houses that didn't
get a church. The church was situated on high ground. The
church was oriented east–west. At first, many of them were
what's called steeple-less churches, but then they were given
towers: 'Thy mercy, O Lord, is in the heavens.'[2]

Now there are churches everywhere. They point people
in the direction of the place they belong. On the west coast,
they trace the Golden Section across the broad windswept
flats; they stand out on the wooded dunes and tower benignly
over the villages. If they haven't been swept to sea. After
a thousand years, the churches have become part of the
landscape's essence, and today is going to be about frescoes.
Or it's going to be about art. Or about the things that go
untouched by time. But before Signe and I turn off towards
our first church, I need to correct a misapprehension:

There was no wave of reformist iconoclasm in Denmark.
Many Danes believe we were initially Catholic, decorating
the inside of our churches with whimsical and instructive

cartoons. Then we became Protestant, which we celebrated by reaching for the whitewash and brush. It's true that in Holland they were terrified of image-worship and did celebrate the Reformation in this manner, but Danish frescoes were intended to be edifying. They were called the Bible of the Poor, or *Biblia pauperum*, and by poor they meant 'poor in spirit'—in other words, the ordinary, unlettered people. These were in no short supply in Denmark, so it wasn't until the seventeenth and eighteenth centuries that the whitewash brushes were finally deployed. The paintings were getting worn, and people were beginning to find them primitive. Tastes had changed: nowadays everything had to be white. In the nineteenth century, people developed a soft spot for history and started uncovering the paintings again. We've been working on it ever since.[3]

'It's just madness,' says Signe. 'What on earth got into them?'

The wind rocks the car.

'Poverty of spirit and the vagaries of fashion,' I say.

'Like an idiot and a poser holding hands,' says Signe.

We're deliberately approaching the frescoes with a certain affected ignorance. We haven't done much research into the churches before setting out to pester priests, church wardens and sextons—and on a Sunday, at that. We want to meet the master who drew and told stories on the walls somewhere between five hundred and a thousand years ago, as though he weren't lost to time.

We turn off towards the Old Parish Church, settled like a beautiful white laying hen at the end of a gravel road near Ringkøbing Fjord. There it's been, among flocks of migrating geese and the whims of time, for more than nine hundred years. There are choppy waves on the fjord. A forest of reeds is torn around in wild patterns by the wind.

We make our way into the church and underneath the obligatory model ship hanging from the ceiling—a beautiful example by the name of Ruth.

'My mother's name is Ruth,' I tell Signe, but she's already found the frescoes further up the church. On the north wall is the type of painting we've set out to find. There she is: an extraordinarily fine and delicate woman, in the middle of an old comic book. Posed contrapposto, she is clad in a gorgeously draped garment that she draws gently to her. Her face radiates openness, compassion and trust. She steals the show.

'I left my sketchbook in the car,' says Signe, taking the key.

Outside the church, the weather is fierce; inside is this figure, her serenity augmented by the storm. She is self-contained, her face free of disquiet, soft. What have they seen, the battered, wind-blasted eyes that have come to rest on her over the centuries? And when did they hang Ruth up there, I wonder, glancing up at the model ship. And then Signe is back. She's got the sketchbook open. First, she gets up close to the fresco. Then she makes straight for the pulpit. I sneak after her, while Signe tries out the master's line. From the pulpit, I can see through the large window. The fjord is churning outside.

'He loved drapery,' says Signe after a period of silence with the wind and the squeaking pen. 'He was pleased they let him paint her dress. This is a sheer labour of love. He's sincere,' says Signe.

'Christian Dior?' I joke.

'Yeah, who knows,' answers Signe, vanishing back into her sketchbook.

She's following the master's drawing of Mary's face—for it must be her, we agree. She's in a richly illustrated retelling of her life, death and ascension.

'That could almost have been drawn yesterday, don't you think?' I ask.

'Yeah. He's stuck around in that line. The result is time-less,' says Signe, as we come down from the pulpit. 'Yes, there's something timeless in the line,' she decides, walking out of the church while I stand still for a minute. I write in my notebook:

'The heavenly mother is resting in a contrapposto pose. They've put Ruth in the rafters. Centuries of eyes on Mary's face. It's all going to be fine. The line is timeless.'

⚜

The sea is on our left again; we're driving north. We're off to visit Staby Church, one of the most important churches in Denmark's cultural heritage. A service has just finished when we arrive, and people are still wishing each other a pleasant Sunday. We take a look at the church from the outside. There are tender four-leaf-clover-shaped windows in its famous apse, but better still are the granite columns

with capitals that breathed the life of the African savannah
into Staby around the year 1200. Two lions, even though one
of them looks more like a monkey, but they had never seen
a lion, so how could they know. A couple of churchgoers
with lovely short grey haircuts drive past us, and we meet
the priest at the door. We apologize for not coming to the
service, explaining that we're on another quest.

'For frescoes?' he asks, gripping his robes firmly, the way
Mary at the Old Parish Church held firmly onto hers. It's
the wind. It's trying to get up underneath him.

'We're on a kind of quest for things that transcend time,'
I say, as Signe strides purposefully through the porch and
into the church. I find her with her face turned towards the
big fresco on the north wall. The verger is pottering about,
extinguishing candles and switching off hearing loops. He
has the nicest face and a key to the sepulchre. I'd like to
go. I know that in addition to some rich and desiccated
corpses in black coffins, the chapel has some ancient runes.

The verger unlocks the sepulchre for us.

'Are the skeletons still down there?' asks Signe, pointing
at the tombs.

'Yes, or they might be mummified,' I say, remembering a
cat we once found behind some boards in my dad's workshop, stone dead but still fur-coated. 'Anyway, the most
important thing in here isn't the dead,' I say. 'The most
important things are those.'

I point at the runes. Carved and painted red, they're to
the left of the door that was once meant for women—the
one they were allowed to walk through for the services.
This was also the door that inducted them back into the

congregation after births and menstruation. 'In the name of Mary, step inside and be clean,' it says, according to the verger, who's just saying goodbye.

I trace my fingers over the runes. They're oddly beautiful, powerful in their age, but at the same time they make me angry.

'Bunch of old arseholes,' I say, and Signe says she feels like glueing a used pad underneath the runes. Still, we agree it is beautiful. That those women had Mary. That they were able to see themselves made divine in her form.

'And speaking of Mary...' Signe says, slipping past me with her sketchbook, drawn towards a remarkable fresco on the north wall. Silence has descended on the church. The dead make no noise, and Signe is settled in a pew, drawing. I pour us a cup of coffee, open my notebook and look up.

The subject?

On the left is a large, beautiful and sulky Virgin Mary with red hair. In the middle are the Three Kings, wild, awkwardly in profile, with King Balthazar on the far right. From Africa. Painted by an unnamed master in West Jutland in 1545, and I can hardly stop looking at him. Balthazar, that is. The coastline is European, but it runs deeper. The culture of the coast has always revolved around migration and ethnic interchange. The Vikings, the drovers, the pilgrims, the travelling merchants, the hosiers. Those who walked and those under sail. A thousand years ago, you could sail these inland waters, along fjords, streams and coves, protected from the savage sea.[4] Even here, among the animals in the savannah and Balthazar in Staby.

'I can barely put it into words,' says Signe after a quarter of an hour, 'but this was painted by a great artist. I mean, I know the proportions are off, he couldn't get the profiles right, he's naïve, genuinely naïve, but he imparted this wild sensuality and energy to the paintings. He's taken such pains over it, like a child sitting down at a kitchen table to draw something difficult. It's sheer joy. A world heritage,' says Signe, and we're silent.

I see what she means. I also see that two artists—a man whose name remains erased by time, and another, who has just come through the women's door—are sitting here together. They're meeting right now. Five hundred years, and they cannot be kept apart. She knows what absorbed his attention then. Jesus's ribs, for example.

'I could spend all day in here,' says Signe. 'Do we need to move on yet?' she asks, and I pour her another half a cup of coffee.

'We'll stay a bit longer,' I say, although we do need to move on to church number three, where the verger has unlocked the door especially for us.

While Signe, still holding her pen, keeps talking to her new friend on the wall, I write in my notebook: 'Jesus's ribs represent the development of an idiom. In Mary's name, step inside and be clean. Women's doors.'

⚜

'Where are we going now?' asks Signe as we cruise towards Thorsminde and up further north. The green and sandy dunes on our left, Nissum Fjord on our right, expanding inland in reflected light.

'Dybe Church,' I say, and after the long panoramic drive, American-style, we take the turning to it. Well, we take the turning towards it, but then I accidentally drive past it and onto a patch of tarmac. I stop in front of a big old red building, and get the powerful sense I've been here before.

'I know this place,' I say.

The church is right behind us. This is its neighbour, a disused school.

'I came here as a child,' I say. 'Or my mum did, and then the rest of us did for a while too.'

I had almost forgotten it, the school with the funny name. The wind sweeps over it. Tall trees rain twigs around it: Dybe School—literally, 'Deep School'. My mum wanted to go to art college when she was young. Only, as a girl from a south-west Jutland farming family in the 1950s, she couldn't. It was her brothers who were allowed to get an education. She and her sisters were supposed to get married and become mothers. But she found herself an apprenticeship and trained as a hairdresser. She wanted to be independent, even if she wasn't much interested in finger waves, haircuts and village gossip.

She ran her own salon for many years, even after she got married and became a mother. But when I was eight, she hung up her scissors. This was the 1970s. There was freedom and self-actualization, as they called it, in the air, and the school was home to an artist, Jonna Sejg. When I was eight years old, my mother went to stay with Jonna for a week.

Coming home, she painted constantly. Later she retrained to teach oil painting, ceramics and drawing. She did illustrations for the newspaper. I was proud of her. And a little afraid of Jonna. She was the first Copenhagener I'd met, and she hugged people. You just didn't do that in Jutland—but Jonna wore big smocks and hugged people. When we went to visit, my dad said to my mum in the car on the way up:

'Do you think she'll want to get all touchy-feely with me again?'

She did indeed. She hugged him till he creaked.

We're standing right by the car, Signe and I. Jonna is dead. The inner warmth of the school is gone; the rot has taken over. My mother's past eighty and still paints and draws, but art college was never to be.

'It was the kind of place where there were always sweets on the table, and you never had to ask permission to eat them,' I say to Signe, and I'm eager to explain that I've just inadvertently driven the car up to a landmark. But Signe has set a course for the church. The frescoes. They're why we've come. The choir is supposed to be packed with them, and so it is.

In Dybe Church, the frescoes are kept behind a gigantic glass door in the chancel arch. We're on the rough part of what's known as the Iron Coast, named for all the ships broken along that stretch. There's always salt in the air; the salt damages the paintings. No mercy outside, but here in the choir it's granted often. Signe lies down in front of the stone altar. Her knees are bent towards the crucifix. It's the paintings that matter here. She can only see them if she lies down on her back. They fill the vaulted ceiling of the choir. There are leafy vines, fabulous creatures and birds of paradise, immaculate coils of vegetation. Flowers unfurling, peacocks strutting and grapes jostling out among the foliage. It's paradise, despite the crucifixion scene depicted alongside: three crosses, Jesus in the middle, and the two thieves. The one on the right is especially difficult to look away from.

'Bit of a dandy, that thief,' I say, lying down next to Signe so that I, too, can see the beautiful birds.

'Must be a self-portrait,' says Signe. 'The guy who painted this has flair.'

She's seen what she wanted and clambers past the altar towards the wall. Taking out her sketchbook, she explains her suspicions. Meanwhile, I'm still lying down. I can't get my mother's rebellion out of my head. This is the first time it's dawned on me that that's what it was. Like lying down in front of an altar and saying, 'Time's up!'

I sit up.

'He's developed a style,' says Signe. 'He's skilled enough at painting branches, birds and vines, sure, but he's boring. He's good at this ornamental stuff. Maybe he had a workshop and sent apprentices. It's wallpaper art.'5

Signe demonstrates, pen to paper, how monotony intrudes on the style, adding that she likes the strange men best.

'You mean Jesus and the thieves?' I ask. 'Yeah, them,' says Signe. 'I'm hungry.'

'Me too,' I say, pointing up at the vaulted ceiling. 'It's all those grapes.'

Then Signe snaps the sketchbook shut around a couple of birds of paradise and slips past me. I follow a minute later, but I pause by one of the pews and look back on my way out. There she sits. She loves silence, so she's sat down in the church. She's in one of the front pews. Far away from her family, she's taking a moment alone before paradise.

I walk back and slide into the pew beside her. We're the same age now. Our hands look similar, and I put mine over hers.

Signe and I get coffee at the café in Bovbjerg Lighthouse. I went up the tower quite recently. The view was as you'd expect from a lighthouse; but then again, Bovbjerg is already so high above the water that you might as well be standing on the cliff itself. South of the tower, the line of maximum extent marks 'this far and no further'.

About eighteen thousand years ago, the place where we're ordering two organic rolls with cheese was underneath a gigantic Scandinavian glacier. It came from the north-east, stopping here on its journey. Then it began to melt. It melted till the water was pouring. Today the cliffs are what's left, the gulls. The fierce gale. Somewhere on the slope, a German tourist has had to give up on flying his drone. We thank the weather for that, even though the wind has pushed him and many other people into the café. We're tucked under the rafters in the keeper's cottage, eating our rolls, drinking coffee and fizzy water. A group of amateur artists is exhibiting its work on the walls. Content-wise, the pieces look like the kind of thing my mother's students used to do. Copies, sunsets. There she'd sit, well liked and talented, teaching them to use shadow as they talked to her about their joys and woes. A bit like patrons at the hairdresser's. The power of compassion, the force of gravity.

'When it comes to art, things have been going rapidly downhill since the twelfth century,' says Signe, pointing at a picture of a ship in distress. 'And no matter what church we see next, it will never measure up to Staby.'

⚜

We've got to put this to the test, so after lunch we set off from the lighthouse towards Ferring Church. We talked about going for a walk on the beach today, but the sand stings our faces and the salt sticks gluily to everything, including the windows of the car. When seen from the lighthouse, the water's colossal surface looks like a grey-green living creature that cannot lie still. As though something underneath, deep down, wanted to make its inner nature manifest.

'Traditionally, the sea is a woman and the sun is a man,' I say. 'Wonder what they're bickering over today.'

'Power, I suppose,' says Signe, and we drive half a mile north along the gravel road to Ferring. I don't tell her about my mum and her attempts to liberate herself. It sticks like a lump in my throat, though our fresco tour is supposed to be a happy memory, and then we're at the church.

It's in the middle of its windswept village. We take a walk around. It's still clinging on, although the edge is fraying. On the green lawns are hastily decorated graves. White picket fences have been built around the small plots of land allotted to the dead. The etched aesthetic makes the overall impression graphic. Enhanced by the light, the sea and the distant horizon, the church shivers with raw and understated beauty.

'I could just sit down and draw here if it wasn't so windy,' says Signe, and I point towards the other side of the road. Almost at the very edge of the cliff is painter Jens Søndergaard's old summer cabin, now a museum. He ended up living there. Unable to escape the sea, dependent on the horizon. Denmark's answer to Edvard Munch, he is absolutely a match for the Staby master when it comes to putting energy into his work, but without the same fidelity, and we don't have time for Søndergaard today. We're here for the fresco. It takes up the whole north wall. There are horses involved, I know.

⚓

And there are, and Signe falls silent. She sits down in a pew, hunched into her drawing space. Lifting my gaze, I see the horses, which are probably donkeys, with their soft muzzles, rounded haunches and long, elegant legs. He was fond of them. And the human faces: full and good. He so wanted to give them speech, but the speech bubble hadn't been invented yet. In the middle, right behind one of the donkeys, is a tree that looks like an underwater plant, like seaweed, its foliage round and bubbly. And the generations of salt-ravaged, sea-dwelling Jutlanders? What have they seen? A horse like the one back home. A tree like seaweed on the beach. Don't be scared. It'll all be fine.

'He loved those animals,' I say.

'Yes,' says Signe, 'and he wanted to tell a story.'

We are quiet, side by side in the church on the edge of the sea, while the master speaks. He tells us of senses and longing. He turns his soft face towards us. He is a human being, coming timelessly towards us. What he says, he says clearly. Nothing has been lost, despite the peeling and the interfering conservators. He is here, just as he was here; and we are here, as we have always been. The storm is here. The silence at the altar, and perhaps there's a small mirror behind it. It's screwed firmly into the back, so that the priest, who is now a woman, can pin her braid properly onto her head. Brush a hand across her brow, examine her face on Sunday morning. Now she draws her garment around her. Her hip outthrust, she steps in front of the congregation. Speaks.

'I could just sit here and draw,' whispers Signe.

'That's exactly what you are doing,' I whisper back.

'Yeah, but I could sit here longer.'

'Then we'll keep sitting,' I say, and we do.

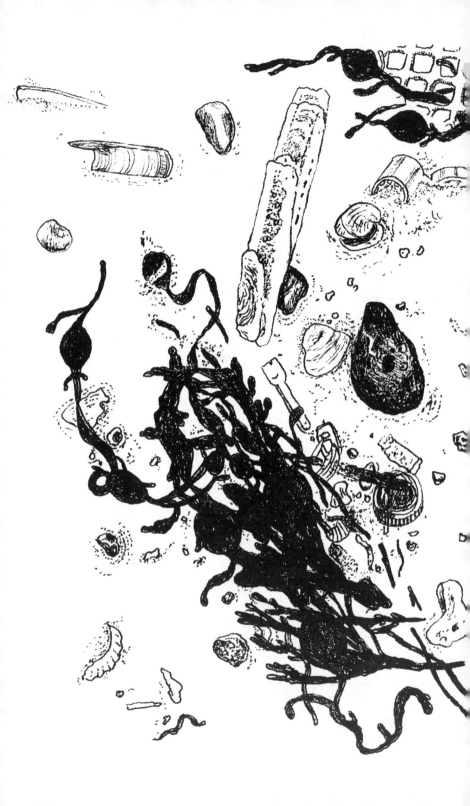

Amsterdam,
Hvide Sande

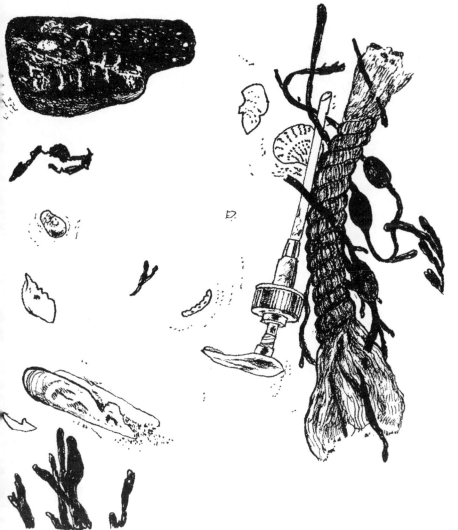

One day, last autumn, I took a walk around Hvide Sande, a town on the central west coast of Jutland. Specks of mizzle on my face, the fjord grey and foggy. It had been stormy a few days earlier, but now the wind had gone east. Along the coast, the sea couldn't be bothered to pick up. Everything seemed oddly latent. The swell was slow and rhythmic, barely visible, like a cat flicking the tip of its tail. The sea has no language, as such, but every once in a while I think it speaks. I passed through Hvide Sande harbour, continuing further and further south. Occasionally a bottle drifted ashore, then a rubber glove, then a dead fish, then a fish crate, nets, balloons. After a storm, the number of birthday balloons explodes in the rubbish that the sea throws up onto the beach. As though blind drunk. A dead seal, millions of small plastic beads. A type of insulation, fragments of polystyrene foam, Jesus sandals and safety boots. Anything that can fall overboard. Anything you throw away. No one really bothers much about it. Now and again there's also a bird; wings at its sides, head craned backwards, beak open in silent song.

I found no amber. Amber and amber-sized chunks of wood are the last natural things to be vomited up after the storm. They appear once the sea relents, and I walked back and forth south of the seaward entrance to Hvide Sande. The wind turbines by the harbour turned lazily. Refuse had piled into fringes along the mountainous dunes, as far as the eye could see. In a few days, the coastal warden would pick up the worst of it. On a good Sunday, the scouts arrive. Bins have been provided for anyone who can be bothered to make a little effort. But that's a drop in the ocean; and what would it say, the ocean, if it could talk? What would its voice sound like, I wondered, watching one grey swell follow another. It was tired; no, expectant, and it was trying to reach up and kiss my shoes.

'Here you have me,' it said. 'Here you have my salt teeth. Your future is rising to meet you.' There was a bottle in the swell. 'You and your consciousness of death. You and your fascination with tools,' said the sea, trying to spit on my trousers. That was after the first storm. The sea gave me wet shoes, it pushed me away, pulled me back, and now I'm far away. I've travelled south of the line, crossing several borders. This autumn I'm living and working in Amsterdam, a long way from Hvide Sande. Such a well-or-dered place, Amsterdam; and there's this small picture in the Rijksmuseum. It's hanging in a not especially splendid room on the second floor—room 2.27, to be precise. It was painted by a man by the name of Gerrit Adriaensz. Berckheyde, and it's empty. Resting. Like something caught just at the moment when you're not sure what it might become.

The painting depicts the Herengracht, one of the five big concentric canals laid out in semi-circles that constitute central Amsterdam. I live and work on the Spui, so I take daily walks along the Herengracht, and I often pause by the painting in room 2.27. It looks like somewhere I know, yet it doesn't because the canal is bare in the picture. The magnificent houses carry themselves proudly upright. They are newly built, still smelling of mortar, putty and varnish. Scented like expensive silks and spices from the East Indian colonies, Java, Bali, Sumatra and others. The Dutch are formidable merchants and sailors. They sail colonial masters and slaves to the West Indies and wares back home to Europe. Amsterdam is growing, and it's a day in the late seventeenth century. The sun is shining. The canal curves faintly, guided by a pair of compasses. It's all so new in the old painting, the water dutifully reflecting the palaces of its tea-trading masters. It is held in place by a town planner. The people stroll along the canal, small and staidly bourgeois. It's all new-won, you can tell, and now it's old and October.

I come to a halt on one of the bridges across the canal. It must be around this point that Berckheyde stood when he found his subject. A light drizzle has set in. It dots my face, small, soft prickles. Not umbrella weather yet, and I keep walking along the Herengracht. I pause underneath a tree. A canal boat drifts by, and behind it the water closes in, flattens out. It's replaced every night while people sleep. I struggle to comprehend how they do it, as the drops play lightly on the surface—small, unassuming circles in an orderly universe.

That Hvide Sande exists in parallel with Amsterdam is difficult to fathom in my nice shoes. Everyone is friendly here, cosmopolitan-minded and willing to chat. Amsterdamers know that there's no trade without conversation, so I talk to people on the street, in shops; I'm asked who I am, and telling them is of no consequence. But in Hvide Sande I'm cautious about approaching people. Best not to say too much, to always weigh my words. Don't want to put a foot wrong. Don't want to sound stuck-up, because I don't want to be stuck-up—but which language am I supposed to use in which world? How can one leave things between the lines in one place yet let them roll off the tongue elsewhere? In Hvide Sande my voice is nervous, but then again I'm safe by the sea. And in Amsterdam I sound like myself, but I'm worried about the canals.

I grew up in a silent culture in a desolate parish full of farmers and seamstresses. The grown-ups were taciturn. They liked to keep themselves concealed from the other adults, but no one hid from the eyes of children. In the homes I entered, I saw and heard the mismatch between the spoken and the truth. It was a matter of protection. If the neighbour got wind of what you were hiding, you might not be able to borrow his combine harvester. And the grain had to be harvested. But I longed for the grown-ups to express themselves, and so literature struck me as a miracle when I found it. I set out to learn this deep language, but when I travelled from the big cities to the distant coast, now in the middle of my life as an author, my language was not always unwelcome.

When I'd been living by the sea for a couple of years, a wolf wandered in from Germany and up through Jutland to live and breed in the deserted areas along the coast. It was wandering, in other words, through the area where I had settled down, and the fear of wolves, the anger, spread frenziedly. There was talk of taking the law into one's own hands, of hatred towards Copenhagen and the EU. It was the fault of those in power that the wolf had come, and this scratched at the wound that existed between the visible and those made invisible.

Danish radio got hold of the story and drove the long road from the capital to my doorstep with a microphone. They asked if I had anything to say about the fear of wolves, and I said it was a matter of public sentiment. You were more likely to be mowed down by a tractor in these parts than eaten by a wolf, I said. Into the microphone. On national radio.

And then I disappeared. So did the man who was painting my woodshed. The woman at the end of the sunken lane didn't give me any biscuits for Christmas. People stopped saying hello when they passed in their cars. I asked a nice old lady nearby how long I would be invisible before my sentence was served. I said it as a joke, but she answered, 'A year and a half.'

And I was invisible for a year and a half, and by the time I gradually turned visible again, I had decided my voice was more important to me than being present in the local community; and of course I love the landscape. I love the dialect, the humour, the helpfulness, but when I need to talk I drive to other parishes, to speak to other people who don't belong. I journey out into the world, and this autumn I'm staying in Amsterdam. Here my neighbour has no combine harvester, so I can say what I like. It's a good thing too, because when I'm forced into silence, language starts to rise menacingly inside me. Like water behind a dam, like persistent climate-catastrophic rain, so seen from language's perspective, being in Amsterdam is safe. The city lets talk flow freely. But water it holds in check.

So far back in history that the details are sparse, the Dutch lived in and off the water. By necessity, at first, in capricious spans of marsh and tidal flats; until they learnt to make something of it. Their knowledge grew, as did their confidence, and they've controlled the water ever since, on a grand scale. They dam, they divert. They want living land, and they take it from the sea. One third of Holland is below sea level. Nieuwerkerk aan den IJssel is 22 feet below.

It takes big dams and nerves of steel. The dams are on the rise by the coast; denial is on the rise among the population. In certain spots along the Dutch shore, the dams are so high and so asphalted that the herring gulls have learnt to open mussels on them. Up into the air with the mussels, then they come smack down onto the dam. Nip down to pick it up, bring it back, then down it goes onto the dam again, until the shellfish opens. The dam withstands it. It has to withstand it. The entire country, the nation, depends on it, and if you head further south-west towards the vast delta, where the Rhine, Meuse and Scheldt flow into the North Sea, you'll find the Delta Works, a series of immense structures designed to protect the floodplain from being engulfed by the sea. Rivers break their banks; rough storms sweep ashore. More rainfall is expected in the future. 'Here you have me. My endless salty kiss. Your future is rising to meet you.' But Holland has civil engineers, and so I stand with my spring tide of language by the canal in the spitting rain.

It's a miraculous balance, I think. Those who live by the water are under constant threat from it. In return, the water gives them access to the world, to trade, to riches. The Danes, like their watery siblings to the south, the Dutch and the Frisians, have been living this way for thousands of years. Vikings, then the merchant fleets, wars. Then the trade triangle: rifles, gunpowder and spirits packed onto a ship in Copenhagen, a dangerous journey across Skagen and down the west coast, then further south to the Gold Coast in Africa. Unload, load with enslaved people, cross the Atlantic to the West Indies in your floating hell. Unload, load with sugar-cane syrup, tobacco and mahogany, then head home to Denmark and count your money.

Living with the water and off the water takes arrogance and submission at the same time. Profit is growth. At stake is life, and I watch tiny droplets adding to the Herengracht, meeting no opposition, and I think of Hvide Sande. How it feels in your body when a storm comes ashore. It's like the water doesn't want to cede power, and the land doesn't want to put up with any more violence. So they fight, and then they reconcile, then they are whipped up once again. The sluice gates resist, the people resist. They build houses that can't be blown away: aerated concrete, square concrete elements, small salt-greasy windows. How safe it seems, Amsterdam, the water-controllers' mecca. So pretty, compared to Hvide Sande. Squatting on its thin longshore bar, Hvide Sande is growing. It's not pretty. It couldn't care less about pretty. It can box your ears and show you the place on the pier where the gulls throw up. It skins fish in its big square halls and houses. Gets tattoos, drinks beer or communion wine and walks stooped against the wind. It's all its own, wild and morose, entirely its own, and pinched on both sides by water, like the miraculous Delta Works of south-west Holland. The lock at Hvide Sande was, for many years, one of Europe's largest. A miracle in its own right. It's not that the Danes don't have good engineers too, because we do. Rather, it's that the peoples of this coastline have learnt from one another: that the Frisians have long been getting mixed up in our gene pool and our culture, and vice versa. Water connects, but there the cosmetic similarity between Amsterdam and Hvide Sande ends. If Amsterdam is a smart gentleman in a brocade waistcoat, then Hvide Sande is a wind-ravaged, short-haired woman in overalls, smeared head to toe in fish blood.

'Here you have me, my salt teeth.'

Those able to control the water can get rich—they're very much aware of that in Hvide Sande. The city sprang up around the new lock. On one side of the narrow strip of land is the North Sea, with its fish, its routes, undercurrents and merciless storms. On the other side is Ringkøbing Fjord, with its mild waters, good salt meadows, migrating birds and fish. On the eastern side of the fjord, the river Skjern—Denmark's answer to the Rhine, Meuse and Scheldt—pours in. At one point, the Skjern—the most voluminous river in the country—was squeezed into a large canal in a fit of rational madness. Now, thank God, the river has been returned its winding bends and is recovering from the interference of ruler-wielding men. Its waters flow forever, weaving in and out of the landscape. Making it breathe and multiply: a touch of drizzle on your face and on a ridge far inland. Drizzle turns to rain, rain turns to water, and water always finds the lowest point. It becomes a rivulet, becomes a stream, becomes a river and runs towards the fjord. It becomes a fjord and jostles up against a thin strip of sand, beyond which the world is waiting. So it was. So it is still in Hvide Sande, where the local authority welcomes new citizens with the words, 'Welcome to Hvide Sande, where Denmark meets infinity.'

Hvide Sande is said to be Denmark's youngest city. Before the 1930s, access to 'infinity' was at the bottom of the fjord, but the passageway kept getting clogged with sand. This meant flooding for the people in the area, and flooding would not do, so they decided to dig a canal further north, on the thinnest part of the already slender spit of land between the fjord and the sea. They knocked a hole through. Their first attempt went wrong: flooding. Then, however, they decided to control the water, and they put a lock in the gap.

On the one hand, the lock at Hvide Sande was meant to ensure that it remained possible to sail from the fjord to the sea, so the southern part was used as what's sometimes called a chamber lock. The northern, and more dramatic, part was used for drainage. It is an impressively massive wall, but its everyday task is to regulate water levels and salinity in the fjord. When it was completed in 1931, it was a minor miracle, and things now moved swiftly, for they knew they were on to something. Over the next ten years, settlers moved to the new makeshift town on the west coast. A fishing community developed. The place got a local school, expanded accommodation for sailors and a hotel; houses were built, and the fishing fleet grew. Today, nearly a hundred years later, the town is experiencing a boom in tourism, summer cabins, houseboats, paragliders, windsurfers, wealthy fishing kingpins, wind turbines and drill bits. It's growing so fast its joints are creaky. It has burst its banks, serving ice cream by the tub on a slightly tired Thursday in August. A local woman is standing there with a hairstyle like a wolverine. She serves you in German, even if you order the ice cream in Danish. You come, you see, from elsewhere. She hasn't seen you down the local pub, at harbourside parties or the supermarket. So you're a tourist. This is Hvide Sande, and if she doesn't know who you are, then you're a German, and the road north and south is heavy with traffic and incoming euros.

Your language is a marker that determines your fate. Build locks with sluice gates into the gap. Stop the talk, stem the water, although both are the path to freedom. They connect you to infinity. There are lives on the line, but you try to stave off death with the help of engineers and quiet resistance. To the north: the fourteen broad gates and impressive sluices of the drainage lock are lifted and lowered with steel cables and electric motors. To the south: the chamber lock, which can halt all the euro-ferrying traffic when the bridge is raised for a fjord boat setting sail or coming home. Between the two locks is a looming building. It's built in the coarse style of North Sea modernism: salt-strong concrete elements cast with gravel on the surface. Rust dribbling from everywhere and anywhere that rust can dribble. Overly small, misplaced windows, preferably plastic. The overall impression? It's as colourless as possible. Yet the tall building between the locks is distinct from this usual no-bullshit architecture, having glammed itself up by being blue and calling itself the Blue Tower. The tower is where the harbour administration and the Navy Coastal Rescue Service are located. They're the people who usher your boat in and out of the world. They're the people who make sure the water is held in check. They're your rescuers, your friends in need, and last autumn after the first storm, I paused quietly beside the tower as I made my way back to the car. I was trying to catch sight of the people inside, but the windows betrayed nothing. The fjord receded grey-ish-wet in the drizzle, which didn't seem like much yet still had me soaked before long. The water by the gates of the lock was foaming, controlled, as it passed through. The powerful sluices stood guard over the process. The Blue Tower shuddered in the fog, and I walked across the lock to the seaward side. There, German tourists had taken to doing what people do at landmarks all around the world: putting padlocks on grilles as tokens of love. I read a few random names on random padlocks:

Anni & Matze,
Heidi & Harry,
Mik & Lucie.

The last accompanied by an already ancient date when they had stood gazing out across the harbour, the turbines and the drilling rigs that sometimes take a breather by the quayside, rocking. The engagement might have been broken ages ago, but at that moment, there and then, they believed that—like the lock itself—they had a handle on everything. Or maybe they put the padlock there precisely because they knew they didn't have a handle on anything.

Vive & Patrizia,
Mandy & Florian,
'*Hand in Hand ein Leben lang.*' A rusty padlock with the words '*Für unseren Lieben Papi*', followed by the names of the bereaved. A padlock against death, and I remember that lock, even though it's hard to think about death in this Dutch Renaissance idyll. But there it was, the padlock, up in Hvide Sande; I prodded at it, and walked down the steps on the seaward side of the lock. Down there the water was oddly glossy, the flowing currents full of seals. Yes, harbour seals circling in the November-grey water. Now and again they poked their heads up into the drizzle. Then they leant back and opened their mouths, as though sleeping or getting a massage. The lock let saltwater into the fjord. Perhaps, in the current, the seals found food and a break from the rigours of life. They kicked back and relaxed, the seals, and yet in the grey fog and mizzle they reminded me of soppy water dogs with deep eyes one moment and the next of supernatural creatures from some other, darker realm. A single large seal caught sight of me as I walked along the quay. It followed, keeping its head slightly above water. When I stopped to take a photo, it paused not sixty feet

away. We surveyed each other, and all tenderness was gone from its wet head. 'Here you have me. Here you have my salt teeth.' Down there in the water, the seal looked like a sodden demon. A skull with empty sockets, staring at me, sober and assured. I took a picture, and it flipped over, turning as soft and affectionate as a much-loved dog. A seal again, in motion; but then it stopped, staring up out of the current: 'I drew you under,' it said, 'and I pressed into your lungs, so that you would not forget the power of this being.'

I still remember that seal, one year later. Another representative of infinity; and now I'm standing by the canal in the heart of Amsterdam, watching the drizzle turn to rain. The canal does not move, but it does receive hundreds of wrecked bikes every year, closing around them as it conducts those who travel waterborne elegantly around the city. The beautiful seventeenth-century houses are built on foundations of sea trade and slavery. Coastal folk are by nature opportunists, and far to the west are the colossal dams meant to hold catastrophe at bay. Meanwhile, Hvide Sande is taking stock of yet another tourist season. If they're going to grow the tourist trade much more, they'll need to reclaim land. Holland has civil engineers. 'There'll be a solution,' they say. And the gulls sacrifice themselves, the wolves roam, and the seals turn in the water: your future is rising to meet you, and now the rain is picking up. It's the wettest autumn in living memory, and I take out my umbrella. Tomorrow I'll go to the Rijksmuseum again. I'll take up my post beside Berckheyde, in room 2.27. In his world there is nothing yet to fear.

Wadden Sea Suite

It's dark in Huisduinen, south of Den Helder in Holland. I hear from Denmark that the first storm of autumn is drawing in from the North Sea, bringing winds of hurricane strength. It's due to hit the north-west coast back home. On the phone to my dad I told him I was going to the southernmost edge of the Wadden Sea, the vast, enigmatic tidal sea on the Dutch, German and Danish coastline, and he decided my timing was poor.

'But I'm about five hundred miles away from your storm,' I replied, because he's often worried about people moving here and there. His West Jutish roots have a solid hold on him that way. Watching what you say and talking people back into place when they're a tad too keen to move is normal in the West Jutish hinterland. The coast itself is for those lured by the foreign. They've no good soil, so they're quite a sorry lot. But two miles further in, and we reach the hinterland. The hinterland is for those with money in real estate and profitable earth. They come down hard on wanderlust. Say you're at some Christmas market in the hinterland with your gingerbread, and you're making conversation at a stall selling hand-knitted socks:

'So, what are you up to these days?' I'm asked.

'I'm just back from London, actually,' I might say.

'London?! Oh, but that's ghastly,' says the woman serving. 'And you do look a sorry little thing,' she might decide to add.

Big cities, free speech and foreign lures are the work of the devil. Both are a threat to the existing order. The word *bonde*, Danish for farmer, comes from Norse, and means 'settled man'. A settled man is master in his own house and reluctant to move.

What the women were, the *Dictionary of the Danish Language* neglects to mention. Still, one thing is for sure: a person glad to seek out other regions is a defector, an *overløber*, which comes from the German *Überläufer*, and describes a person who has gone over to the enemy. Any time you say you've been to New York, Berlin, Cairo, what you're really telling the hinterlander before you is that you don't think he or she is good enough. My dad's got this same conditioned reflex from his proud West Jutish forebears. One of the times he was most frustrated over my urge to see exotic places was when I moved to Fanø in the Wadden Sea. Fanø is an island, and people who live on such things are encircled by water. That means wanderlust, no question, and anyway—water is dangerous. Ships go down, ferries too. My risk of drowning rose considerably, he felt.

But I lived on Fanø for a year. It was unforgettable. I was besotted with a married man. The married man was besotted with me being besotted with him, and it should have set all the lighthouses along the coast to flashing, but it didn't. He lived far away, I lived in the village of Sønderho at the southern tip of the island, and with every day that passed I was swallowed up more and more in the landscape. The Wadden Sea is powerful, and I lived a far stretch out there. You don't come out the other side untouched.

First, I stayed at Julius Bomholt's House, also called 'the Poet's Place', a big old shipmaster's house owned by Esbjerg Council. It is made available to Scandinavian writers as a retreat and was mine for six months. Yet when it came time to move out, I wasn't done with Fanø. Coming up, I had an extended trip to the USA. The married man was involved. I thought I might as well stay in Sønderho till then, so I took a room with a lovable local woman, in her shipmaster's house. 'Johanne's House', I call it in my memories, because that's what it was: her house.

My year in Sønderho is a cello's sound inside me. I have only to glimpse the chimneys of Esbjerg Power Station and it begins to play. It sounds like an old-fashioned piece, Bach or Pärt. The silent space, a lonely string instrument, and then that long-suffering bending to the wandering of the moon and the clock of the tides. I love the Wadden Sea, though there's something strange and sucking about it, and so I got a train from Amsterdam to Den Helder. There I rented a bike, despite the gusting wind. I wanted to get to Huisduinen and see the sign that marks: here begins the Wadden Sea. If you can say that something so strangely ethereal begins, and you can. You can see with the naked eye where that force takes over. In Denmark the transition is strongly felt along the west coast of Fanø and up towards Skallingen; the infinitely slick and grooved expanses pass from the south into something like a sea, lined with

nearshore breakers. Nearshore breakers: the North Sea.
Wide-flung tidal flats: the Wadden Sea.

Cycling to Huisduinen I saw the transition there too.
Sandflats, lying in readiness, gigantic bars in the agitated water. This is where it begins, then: the Wadden Sea
UNESCO World Heritage Site. The national park ends
somewhere up by Johanne's House, and I wanted to see
this miracle take over from a southern direction.

'You don't want to walk smack into a spinning top like
that,' said my dad on the phone.

'But I'm so far from the storm,' I said. 'It's up near you
lot. Not here.'

But storms have eyes. Their eyes are round, and they
whirr. Grand Hotel Beatrix in Huisduinen has taken me
into its fold. The hotel is located immediately behind the
dam, a burly asphalted hulk, and on the other side of the
northbound highway is the lighthouse, Lange Jaap, casting
its bright cone into the pelting rain and sea foam. There
is a storm blowing in Huisduinen. Lange Jaap sharpens
and resists. Everything is black besides the light, sweeping
rhythmically across the hotel. I've taken cover in my room.
The building shakes. Small fox in the cave's darkness.

Still, I did my best to make it to the dam before nightfall.
I walked south with a scarf over my face. Grains of sand
stinging, eyes watering.

I walked like a slash against the wind, while the sea
toiled against the disaster-proof dam. To the north, Den
Helder, which so oddly mirrors Esbjerg back home, and a
ferry bravely making the short crossing to the island beyond
the town. It could have been Fanø, but it is called Texel.

It's the southernmost of the Frisian islands and Fanø is the northernmost. Island sisters, and I would have been there, but had to settle for seeing it at a distance. And finding the sign, and I found it:

Welkom in het Waddenzee Werelderfgoed Gebied
Welcome to the Wadden Sea World Heritage Site

It's warm here in the Beatrix. I've taken out a map. I'm looking at islands with funny names. To the south are the West Frisians, Texel the first pearl in the chain—or the pot of gold at the end of the rainbow. After Texel come Vlieland, Terschelling, Ameland, Engelsmanplaat, Schiermonnikoog, Rottumerplaat, Rottumeroog, and then the islands known as the East Frisians: Borkum, Juist, Norderney, Baltrum, Langeoog, Spiekeroog, Wangerooge, Mellum. They speak German now, call themselves North Frisian and keep adding and adding, like pearls on a string. Pellworm, Hooge, Amrum, Nordstrand, Gröde, Nordmarsch-Langeness, Oland, Föhr and Sylt. The language transforms slowly with each pearl, and suddenly they speak Danish. They call themselves Rømø, Mandø, Fanø, Langli. The chain is intact. No border can sever it.

It ought to be silent here, I think under the duvet, listening to the fury outside. Silence and a stringed instrument.

The Wadden Sea is one large violin body, which the water plays a few times a day, rising and falling, rising and falling. That's how I pictured it the year I lived there. This silent suite was broken only by the fire alarm. In Sønderho on the southern tip of Fanø, it went off at noon every single

Saturday. For there are three things they fear in Sønderho: shipwrecks, storm surges and fire. The town of shipmasters is thatched: each house, except for a few lone contrarians, is oriented east to west. And thatched. Around them filters a system of paths and orchards. The idyll is absolute, Grade I listed. So every Saturday at noon, the fire alarm went off. That way you knew it worked should all hell break loose.

And then came the women. Since the siren was going off at twelve every Saturday anyway, they thought they might as well see it as a signal to summon the tribe. They slipped out of their gloriously painted shipmasters' houses. They walked down Landevejen and Nord Land, Øster Land, Sønder Land, Vester Land. They darted, scurried and strode down tangled paths through Sønderho, paths laid down by the coffee-thirsty. They steered a course for the pub, where a long table was set out for them. The stocks of draught beer and white wine had been kicked up a notch. The coffee machine was switched on and the Brøndum Snaps was laid out (Rød Aalborg is for the mainlanders) because there had to be booze-laced coffee too, to keep everything going. And there they sat, the women of Sønderho. They settled their broad backsides around the table, becoming their own version of fire. Gossip set ablaze.

A kind of matriarchy, yes. Historically speaking, a small community where women held power. When the people of Fanø bought their island from the king in the mid eighteenth century, they also bought their freedom and the right to international sea trade.[1] They didn't wait to be told twice. In Sønderho, the men purchased big ships, declared themselves shipmasters and set out like the Frisians they were to trade across the seven seas. They got a long way, the men of Fanø. They brought riches home. The shipmasters' houses grew, flourished, acquired fantastical colours, garrets, windowpanes and extensions. Sønderho transformed into a miraculous village, a community at once isolated and international in the middle of a wayward sea. Sometimes the men were away for months. Other times they set out on long voyages and were away for years at a stretch before they came home. If they did come home, that is, for ships go down, and here's how the situation worked out for Sønderho's women:

Your husband is at sea most of the time. When he comes home, if he comes home, he gets you pregnant. On top of that, he must be occupied somehow. If he's busy painting the outside of the house, he won't be underfoot inside. So you put him to work.

'Why don't you paint stripes above the windows, my friend,' you say.

It takes time, and meanwhile, everything carries on much as before. You're used to running things. You farm. Keep animals. You, the children, the other women and the old men help each other when he's away. Sometimes you go too.[2] Sometimes you join your husband, your brother, your father, and see the world. But back home, it is you who decides when the hay should be harvested.

This is how it was. They settled things for themselves, the women, by and large. Decisions great and small, including those on behalf of the village; they took care of it all. Which was fine, and she looked forward to him coming home. Even though it was a hassle, his restlessness, the power struggles and uncertainty. Four or five such years can turn a spouse into a stranger, near enough. And again he had to be off. Gather, scatter. Gather, scatter.

If he did not come home, that, too, was dreadful. Then she was a widow in a village of many widows and unmarried women. But the widows and the spinsters moved in together. They took care of one another and the children. They drew an ingenious system of paths between the houses and the homes of the elderly with their feet. A cottage industry sprang up, dealing in mutual care, preserved fruit, salted fish, gossip, social control and money. While the straightening of the river Skjern shows what a landscape looks like when someone's been at it with a spirit level, you should take a look at Sønderho to see how paths arrange themselves under women's feet: organic as the roots of trees.

The sign of Fanø's matriarchy was their dress. Fanø's men just wore clothes: wooden shoes, boots, *wadmal* and a cap. But Fanø's women wore a uniform. It hadn't emerged out of thin air—it had immigrated from the south, like their architectural style, their genes, their merchant zeal. In other words: it was Frisian. If you disregard the trading town of Ribe, where you could sell your fish, Fanø was more oriented downwards, towards its sister islands, than towards the Danish mainland.

At the top was a scarf called a cloth. Its bow had to be knotted in a particular way that made it look like a sail. Frisian woman: sailor-wife. There was no shortage of skirts, because it was important to create wide hips underneath a narrow waist. The jacket was buttoned up if you were unmarried. If you were married, a single button was left undone. There were various versions of the garments appropriate for various phases of life. Little girls learnt at around seven years old to tie their cloths, initiating them into the tribe. The women's garb was roughly the same colour as the houses, so in principle it was her he mended if he came home. And if he came home, they danced together. They danced one of the most beautiful traditional dances on earth: the *sønderhoning*.

It really has to be seen, but this is how it goes: first they walk hand in hand, then he reaches both hands around her, behind her back. Putting one of her arms behind her back, she grabs hold of him. The other arm she places lightly around his body. Then they whirl like scaled-down dervishes across the floor. They have one another caught, in a centrifugal force. Like a North Sea depression, with its silent eye and its wildness at the periphery. He clasps her firmly, as though she were life itself. She allows it, and looks determinedly, not coyly, at a slanting angle to the floor. For he has a solid grip on her, the man, but he does not own her.

The first time I saw a young couple spontaneously take to the floor and dance this dance at the pub one chance night, when someone happened to have brought their violin, I was moved.

'Oh, that's just beautiful,' I said to the others at the table, who then got up and danced too, as though it were a quite ordinary thing one might decide to do at the End of the World one weekday night: to dance a dance so simple and powerful that it has survived for generations. The young people look like it comes to them naturally. I don't know if that can be true, because it's difficult, and where I come from we were forced to dance traditional dances at the community centre, after which we immediately forgot them. There's a community centre in Sønderho too, where they might have been made to learn, so maybe somebody's put them through it. But as adults, it looks like they want to dance it of their own accord. I tried, but the man I could have danced with was absent, and anyway, he had committed to dancing with somebody else.

I wonder how Texel, beyond the hard-boiled dam and the water, feels about the mainland? Was it, like Fanø, reasonably indifferent until it was reduced to a place for holiday-makers and romantics from the capital? Are they still full of wanderlust over there? Opportunistic, die-hard, self-assured? Does the Wadden Sea tug at them the way it tugged at me the year I lived in Sønderho, still young and full of illusions? It affected you, the Wadden Sea and its tidal pulse. The natives knew that. Births got underway as waters rose, they said. Those due to die died when the waters receded. You could read it in the obituaries. So-and-so died late Tuesday night 'at falling tide'. It was important to include that. God was one thing, the Wadden Sea was another, and the two things could scarcely be separated.

I used to walk down Nord Land street every night, up to the dike, listening. The starry sky formed a dome above the island, vast, curved and infinite. As I stood there, I sensed the depth of this curve. Up and down became relative terms, and when I shut my eyes, I could hear the silence of the Wadden Sea, like some kind of resonance. North, the sound of breakers taking over. A deep bass sound of currents and snapping water. But to the south and southeast were the flats, and through the flats ran the enormous underwater trenches, the deeps. These channels and their tributaries, the tideways, ran like juicy veins into the mudlands. Unseen, almighty, they wove quietly in and out, in and out of the Wadden Sea, like blood supplying a placenta. The deepest trenches had been given names, the seriousness of which is understandable—Knot Deep, Grey Deep, Gallows Deep—and the Wadden Sea became a huge basin beneath the vaulted stars, where everything fertile grew, including death. Perhaps the cello's sound was coming from the deeps, from the tideways. Perhaps I'd brought it out there myself. Perhaps it couldn't be any other way.

⚜

The lighthouse rakes its beam across the sea, and I have set the map of the Frisian islands aside. I'm looking at old photographs from Fanø instead. It's safe that way, and what I see in the pictures is the way they carry themselves in nearly all of them, the women. Wrapped in cloths, padded widehipped by their underskirts. Their jackets narrow across their chests, their faces hard as leather. They stand at one end of the house, gazing confidently at the interloper.

These are Johanne's foremothers. They stand in front of sand dunes, swollen orchards and buses. Johanne once told me that her family were Frisians from the south who

had settled on Fanø sometime in the seventeenth century.
They'd been living on the island so long that her grandmother, as a child, had been painted by the well-known
Fanø artist Julius Exner. The portrait hung in Johanne's
living room. Grandma as a little girl, with a pretty cloth,
initiated into the tribe. As I recall, I think there was a cat
in her arms as well. Inside the wardrobe, the grandmother
in the painting had risen from the dead in the form of
traditional Fanø clothing: the clothing Grandma had worn
when she became a grown woman. To Johanne, the clothing
was sacred. Every year on Sønderho Day in July, people told
her she should put it on. She didn't want to. She didn't like
the way the mainlanders and holidaymakers, slightly too
rich and privileged, played dress-up in their foremothers'
costumes. The garments were deeply serious, and not just
something to wear for the festival one day out of the year.
They were dolling themselves up in borrowed plumage, felt
Johanne, and on the whole I thought she was right. The
last Fanø woman to wear the clothing died in the 1970s.
The exodus from the outer periphery to the big cities had
begun. The era of the shipmasters was long over, and so
was the matriarchy. From now on, the women were supposed to have children to keep the local community alive.
The young women on Fanø started to wear miniskirts and
bell-bottoms; they styled their pageboy haircuts with curling
irons. They were wrapped up in the number of pregnancies,
both theirs and other people's: the survival of the school,
of the greengrocer's. But the city slickers wanted to have
their fun with the passing of time. They played at the old
days, marched in processions through the city with cloths

bristling and hips rolling. Johanne, sweet person that she was, put up quiet resistance. 'Grandma's clothing' was not to be sullied by vapid tourism or people who didn't understand what it meant.

For it meant more than just power. It meant longing, hard graft, vulnerability. And it meant that you lived with the Wadden Sea, in birth and in death. That you realized what those great flats gave—life and rich growth, wildfowl, glasswort, amber—and what they took from human life. Grief came with the privilege of wearing the clothes, and that coffee laced with schnapps wasn't just about standing one's ground stoically against the cold. It was also medicine to combat the forces of Gallows Deep.

In the storm outside, between Texel and Den Helder, are the underwater rivers of Marsdiep and Nieuwediep, and somewhere near the harbour you might run across a pumping station called De Helsdeur, 'Hell's Gate'. They understand, the West Frisians, that this landscape is bountiful one minute and all-consuming the next. It is the job of Hell's Gate to try and keep hubris at bay. I hope it holds tonight while I look at pictures. There's one of a Fanø woman by her neat picket fence. There's one of a Fanø woman with her daughters in tow. There she stands where she can, and she's in the centre. In one of the pictures you sense her presence to an almost supernatural degree. It was taken on Fanø Beach one February day in 1915. A group of women in Fanø dress have gathered like cormorants in the cold. Maybe they're posing for the photographer, their cloths fluttering in the wind. Maybe they're making sure nobody gets any closer. Behind them is an enormous

sagging German zeppelin by the name of *L3*. It has just
caught fire, and as the women stand there, they seem to be
keeping watch over the burning. Only the day before, this
zeppelin had been a giant, making its way from Hamburg
to Skagerrak to scout for British submarines. There was a
war on, of course. And then came the south-west storm.
It set in with snow. The zeppelin drifted in the wind, the
engines battling to no avail. Half an hour north of the
German border, the last one gave out. An emergency landing in neutral territory on Fanø was their only resort. From
the safety of the beach, the Germans shot a flare into the
airship, setting it alight. Flames and curiosity had drawn
these women. They are of another world, standing there.
No, they were of another world.

I don't know what Johanne thought when the fire alarm
went off every Saturday, gathering the women of Sønderho
at the pub for a drink and a gossip. I think she thought it
was nice. She used to go along, at any rate. At Johanne's
house, I'd often sit and chat with her about anything and
everything. Even after I left the island, came home from the
USA and moved to Copenhagen. My wanderlust took over.
The schism in which all identity is formed made me set out.

The water rose and fell, the pulse beating the hours of
the day. I know that good souls around Johanne eventually
prevailed upon her to wear her grandmother's clothes, just
for one day of the festival. If anyone was going to wear
it then, she should be the one. And she was proud of it,
after all, she told me down the phone. She'd felt strong and
beautiful in it, and I wish I could have seen her. But I never
did. The last time I visited Sønderho, it was for Johanne's

funeral. That day no one wore Fanø dress, but the grief, that was real.

Over coffee after the funeral, we sang the song that's always sung at gatherings on Fanø. Gather, scatter. A song that mimics the tides and the comings and goings of the world. A people with wanderlust isn't afraid to sing in chorus:

'The time has come to travel, friend—my path to distant lands I wend.'

My hinterland family would have moaned 'ghastly' to that song. In their circles, they sang, 'The Jutlander, he's strong and tough, and he will not be moved.' But my grandfather's family was full of fjord fishermen, and my great-grandfather was a shipwright in Esbjerg. I have no doubts about my refrain: *Überläufer*.

After the wake and the booze-laced coffee, I walked through Sønderho and out towards the southern tip. It was September, the sky was high, and I pressed on across the flats. I walked in the direction of Gallows Deep, talking to Johanne. I don't know if she died at a falling tide, but I know she had the Wadden Sea so deep down inside her soul that she can't possibly be anywhere but here. And so I stood, listening to the silence some way out, the stringed instrument. Ribe Cathedral a vast omen to the east. Feeling the vault close below me and above, I crouched down. I took a handful of wet sand and let it wring out through my fingers. The Wadden Sea is a living being with a big, damp lung.

'For the men we couldn't count on after all, Johanne. And for the tenderness we felt for them anyway,' I whispered, leaving my handprint in the mud. I could have sat there for a while and seen it erased by the tide. But the tide comes in quickly in these parts, and we must gather, scatter. Welcome and goodbye.

'In My Distress'

A young Frisian from Groningen sets sail from Rotterdam in Holland for Gothenburg in Sweden. It's November 1917. His schooner is called the *Zwaluw*, meaning 'swallow'. It's laden with apples and tulip bulbs, and neither he nor the first mate has taken the navigator's exams. There's no need, they think, for they are Frisians: the water is in their command. So the *Zwaluw* sails. It's heading north. The captain is in his early twenties, and his name is Lieuwe. It's autumn, the North Sea is rough, but the *Zwaluw* got its name because it can travel far and wide. The schooner sails north, while the Dutch dams tower along the coast. He's making good headway, Lieuwe. He sails up past the West Frisian and East Frisian islands. He slips smoothly past Helgoland and plots a course for the west coast of Jutland. He's going to Gothenburg with the apples and the bulbs. He passes Esbjerg at some point and reaches Vejers, Henne. He does not hesitate: he's got to keep going. He's staying well away from the land because he hasn't passed his navigator's exams. Nor has the first mate. Along this part of the line, the Iron Coast, there are no islands to hide behind when the storm comes. And now the storm does come. Now the skies and the sea are one. Now the *Zwaluw* is dashed up against the sandbars, and those are dangerous. If the ship runs aground on one of them, it's a disaster. The violent breakers around the sandbars pulverize grounded vessels, and the experiences passed down from their forefathers are not enough. Lieuwe and the first mate battle in vain. First the schooner slams into a sandbar, then it's stuck there, then it's lifted bit by bit towards the coast and ends up near the beach with a frightened crew, apples and tulip bulbs in its hold. It has struck the dune. The sea toys with the ship, like a cat toys with a ruffled bird. The *Zwaluw* is stranded, helplessly stranded, on the beach where a hundred years later I go for walks when I'm at home.

This summer, the first sandbar broke the surface near Vedersø Dune. I saw a rip tide in it. It was a mild day, the breakers were a long way out, and I thought it would probably be fine to let the waves wash over me at that distance. I defied my fear of the Valkyrie waves; or I thought that at that distance I'd have control of them. The plan was to see, from a place of safety, how hard a rip tide could pull. A little wave, a bigger wave, big waves come like death, three at a time. The first big wave approached, broke, washed tenderly over me—but when it went to wash back through the gap, it dragged me with it. Such a peaceful summer's day, crawling ungracefully back to the beach. The sea is still not yours to play with. Your shipwreck is predictable, my friend.

It's thought that more than ten thousand ships have foundered off the west coast of Jutland.[1] The storms sweep

them in, there's no shelter, and the sandbars are full of sucking holes, breakers, undertows and violence. The stormy
forces of the universe clasp their arms around the world.
They clutch deep down inside it. I was sitting in the car
once by the seaward approach to Thorsminde when a hur-
ricane-force gale came ashore. The car rocking, the radio
crackling with news about the water level. And I kept an
eye on the lock as things got dicey. The wall of waves at
the end of the entrance to the harbour. Drab grey on grey,
flying clouds of foam. The word 'mercy' keeps coming to
mind, and I remember the threat of a break in the dam
during the storm of 1981 in Southern Jutland. That was at
the end of November, storm season. I was running around
with a playmate inland, helping her dad catch pigs because
the roof had flown off the barn. They had to be moved, the
pigs. My parents had driven to the summer cabin to check
if the privy was still standing. My mum was also supposed
to draw scenes from the storm for the paper. There were
reports on the radio about a breach in the dam. I was so
afraid of the wind. If it could pick the roof off a barn, if
it could walk through enormous dunes and dikes, what
could it not do?

Late that afternoon, I pushed my bike home without a
word to my friend. But her mum must have called, because
I met my dad halfway home, driving over the hill. I wasn't
supposed to be outside alone in that weather, and 'good
Lord, you reek of pig,' he said once we'd been driving
awhile, but then he comforted me. It's nice being comforted, and now I live with an open windswept expanse
fronting onto the sea. When the storms come ashore from

the north-west, I'm tucked behind the dune forest and my neighbours' gabled homes. But when the storm comes in from the south-west, I can hear its voice. It's coming from a secret place. It's like the roar belongs to the galaxies, and it reduces me to grains of sand. I lie and listen to it in the dark. I can see the wind shaking my chestnut. The tree is used to it. All the trees on the North Sea coast are. They bend, crawl if necessary, but I'm nervous about my roof. I'm afraid the forces will fly off with it. When will I be staring up at the universe? When will I be raised up out of the reality I know and into the next? In the thicket, the wind can snap trees like matches. It sounds like gunshots when fresh wood breaks. It sounds like violence, but violence without the intention of it. Energy in motion, but unruly; the kind you have to give a name. A name binds the unknown to the Earth, so these days we call the storms Xaver, Christian and Herwart: reliable names. There they are in black and white, detached from the wildness of the universe and dressed in practical shoes. Not that they're malicious by nature, necessarily. But they'll make you whisper 'mercy', for once they're underway their will is blind.

This is important to remember. For Lieuwe too. His small act of hubris with the *Zwaluw* has ended in the vengeance of Nemesis on the dunes. It's the 23rd of November 1917. The schooner is on the beach, humiliated. The local coast-guard turns up with a breeches buoy, but neither Lieuwe nor the other crew members know how to use it. They never went to maritime training college: they're Frisians. The Jutlanders are on the beach, yelling gibberish at them. There is gesturing and no time to waste; the rescue operation takes a confusing turn, but in the end it succeeds. The ship is unloaded, the water drops. Watchmen are assigned to the cabin to keep an eye on the cargo. They play cards, and the *Zwaluw* is flat-bottomed. While they're enjoying themselves, the sea lifts the schooner free of the beach. It carries it back out. It strands the *Zwaluw* again. This time, a breach is torn in the hold. Apples and tulip bulbs wash ashore, settling in the lather up and down the coast. The apples taste good, think the folk on the dunes, but supposedly the tulip bulbs weren't touched. The following spring, the beach was full of tulips in blossom. To the south, to the north, Dutch tulips swaying in the wind. It must have been an extraordinary sight, and I imagine them a delicate yellow, the tulips. Yes, yellow and hardy, the kind that's at the bottom of my garden. I bought them with the house. They come every year. I've chosen to hope that not all the tulip bulbs were left pitching in the breakers. And Lieuwe? When ships run aground and sailors are rescued, the common practice is to house them well. So they put the young captain up at the local manor. The owner's daughter, Birgitte, fell in love with him—and he with her, we must assume (for Frisians are coastal folk, coastal folk are survivors, survivors see opportunities, and the house is large and beautiful). Thus, a Frisian was inscribed for all eternity in the church register on the occasion of their wedding in October 1920: 'Bachelor Captain Lieuwe Stienstra, b. 17 January 1896, Son of Oetze Stienstra and his Wife Tallagien de Raad, in Groningen. Resident at Aabjerg in Vedersø.' But the *Zwaluw* had long since sailed on.[2]

It was a miracle that no one from the 'Tulip Ship', as the *Zwaluw* has since been called, drowned. That's down to luck, the relative mildness of the storm and the coastguard. Up and down the coast, besides earning a bit of money from the regular shipwrecks, the locals have been putting their lives on the line for centuries to help strangers in need. You see the old coastguard stations hunkering down everywhere, with their hipped roofs and two criss-crossed Danish flags painted on the gate. Every churchyard testifies that their rescue operations did not always succeed. At some—Harboøre churchyard, for instance—you see that the coastguard suffered the greatest losses. One stone tells of twelve men from the parish who set out one January night in 1897 in a lifeboat, the *Liløre*, to rescue two local fishing boats during a storm. They thought they'd glimpsed a light out on the sea, put the lifeboat in the water, and vanished into the dark. An hour and a half later, the boat drifted ashore upturned. On the memorial stone at the place where their bodies are buried, the inscription bears witness to how young they were.

Elsewhere in the churchyard, there's a memorial wall. It bears the names of the many local sailors and fishermen whose bodies their families could never bury. But they have to be commemorated somewhere, so here they are. There's a verse written for the mourners:

At sea they earned their daily bread
And found there bitter death instead.

When resurrection dawns one day
God grant them life anew, we pray.

So there they stand, the bereaved, trying to picture those
they have lost without letting the most powerful images
take over. For the body is not trivial to them. It ought to
be somewhere, tenderly and soberly stored. Not carried
restlessly by sea currents without a word of scripture at
parting. It ought not to be food for animals. The severed
limbs, the drowning, the disintegration, and who knows,
perhaps a person needs to sublimate the images they can't
escape into a kind of divine thanksgiving. Since death
and the notion of it haunts them. Day in, day out, they
submit to death, to grief, until they celebrate death for the
capacity to live. On many of the gravestones at Harbøore,
death is almost thanked, and I understand the sentiment.
Or rather, I understand the defence mechanism behind
it. For drowning, fate, are ever-present here, and the sea
is always strongest. When you have no means of resist-
ing, and inevitably come out worse off, you ascribe to
the forces that defeat you a wisdom greater than yours. If
Stockholm syndrome exists in religious form, it may well
be in Harbøore, for you are a hostage, and your dead are
at sea. It has taken them, but God has taken them too.
Where one begins and the other ends is not easy for a
small person to tell. Yet He governs all for the best, and
on Laurids Andersen's grave is written:

In my distress I called upon the Lord, and cried
unto my God: He heard my voice out of His

temple, and my cry came before Him, even into
His ears. (Psalm 18:6)

Laurids cries. He cries as the cold settles into his muscles.
He screams until the saltwater flows into his lungs. First,
the water drowns the cry, then Laurids, and then the storm
drowns out everything. Later come the cries of others. They
cannot save themselves. They cry before the gravestones.
They cry in their distress through the storm and far beyond,
into death and to eternal life.

When I was small, I was afraid of waves. I was afraid of
them even before the Valkyrie wave staked a claim to me,
and that didn't exactly make me less afraid. As a child,
I imagined sometimes what it would look like if all the
waves disappeared. A monstrously flat scenario appeared
before my mind's eye. I pictured all the water retreating.
From the dunetops, I surveyed a vast landscape, wrecked
ships clustered in especially dangerous areas where they
often sank. I had seen maps of the wrecks. Caviar maps,
I'd heard them called. They were tacked up everywhere,
making it clear to visitors that although a summer's day out
there might look beautiful, this was still one of the world's
most dangerous coastlines. The crowds of black dots, which
looked like fish eggs, meant death and misery. They meant
washed-up treasure, too, and riches on the beach, but above
all they meant death and misery, and I imagined what the
sea would look like if the sea weren't there. It would be a

never-ending to the Danes. They tried to make it difficult for the British to sail through Danish waters by putting out all the lighthouses and removing all the sea markers, but the British found their way. They sailed in large convoys of merchant ships from the Bight of Hanö in the Baltic Sea, down around the very southern tip of Denmark, up through inland Danish waters, along the Swedish coast, past the town of Skagen in the far north, then south and home to British ports. To protect all the cargo being transported, they assigned them naval guards. In the autumn of 1811, these included the *St George* and the *Defence*, proud ships of the line, which accompanied the convoy between the Baltic and Great Britain. They were colossal vessels, dressed for war and full of sailors, naval officers and people who were more or less voluntarily serving on board. They were armed with cannons. They had sails as big as sports grounds, and they had bad luck along the way. First, they were late leaving with the convoy from the Bight of Hanö. The direction of the wind wasn't cooperating, and the season was turning stormy. Taking a chance, they sailed south around Denmark's lowermost spit of land, but then the *St George* ran aground on a gigantic sandbar. It lost its rudder, but managed to hastily fit the emergency replacement, and the convoy continued on up the Kattegat, crossing east towards Sweden, then up the Swedish coast before seizing its chance and sailing past Skagen, then south along the Iron Coast. There was fear on board and the feeling of a rough storm in the air. And the storm struck. It struck in the form of a lunatic hurricane. This was Christmas Eve, but it showed no mercy. The galactic roar must have sounded right across the coast. People lay uneasily in their houses, thinking of the death and the cargo that would drift ashore in the coming days. Somewhere in the dark, the storm was preparing for its harvest. Hundreds of people, trapped in an incomprehensible hell of monstrous waves, wreckage, damage and sudden death.

On Christmas Day the storm subsided, but by then two jewels of the British fleet had gone down off the coast of Thorsminde and Fjand. And then the corpses began to wash ashore. They were borne in their hundreds, all along the coast, from Fjaltring down to Blåvandshuk. Some washed up fully clothed, others naked. The breakers had been so violent that several of the bodies had been mutilated by the wreckage: the torso of a man was carried in, then a leg, then an arm. At Blåvandshuk the coastal warden found the bodies of two women and a man. A Black man, for Great Britain was a colonial nation, and the list of crew revealed how truly international the navy of the Empire was. But the North Sea does not discriminate on the grounds of nationality, sex or ethnicity. Nor was it too grand to play slaughterhouse with women, children, enslaved people, free as well as unfree men. And so the sea did that night what no war had been able to do to the *St George* and the *Defence*. It defeated them with ease.

Before it foundered, the *Defence* had led an adventurous and triumphant life on the seven seas. It had sailed the English Channel. It had been on expeditions to Gibraltar. It sailed to India and was a flagship during the Battle of Cuddalore. It spent the French Revolutionary Wars in constant active service, including in the Mediterranean, where it took part in battles against the French navy. During the First Battle of Copenhagen, the ship was held on standby north of Middelgrund, the island fort off the coast of Copenhagen, as was the *St George*, whose life as a flagship was no less dramatic. The *Defence* took part in the Battle of Trafalgar and the Second Battle of Copenhagen, and after that this rugged survivor of a warship sailed the convoy through the Baltic and home to Great Britain. Until one night before Christmas, when it took a chance in a hurricane on the Jutish west coast. Seventeen men survived, and despite the war were treated as the shipwrecked always were on the coast: with kindness, warm clothes, good beds and schnapps. Two of them were Americans from Boston and New York. Press-ganged into war by the British, they crawled ashore at Thorsminde; and that same Christmas, that same storm, the British warship the *Hero* was shattered on the island of Texel, north of Den Helder in Holland. More than five hundred men drowned. Another Christmas night, during a North Sea hurricane, more than two thousand people connected to the British navy were swept overboard. Broken masts and cannons hurled at soft bodies, real, living lives dragged down and under. 'In my distress I called upon the Lord,' but it did no good. The storm has a silent eye. At the periphery it rages, and the wrecks, the corpses are deposited on sandbars, hidden from posterity, first as swollen food for eels and later skeletons. A feast for crabs and barnacles. Then those months in the winter of 1812, when bodies washed ashore along the line like dead seals. Mass graves had to be dug, dead man's mountains, in the dunes. The churchyards grew too full, the stench too heavy.

The survivors were half carried into outbuildings and barns or down to the beach, to identify the bodies, if they could. Afterwards, they were helped back to friendly rooms. They were miracles, true exceptions, and they had real men's names: Joseph Page, John Brown, Ralph Teazie, John Platt, Amos Stephens, Thomas Mullins, Michael Collins, John Anderson, William Donald, William Hampson, William Watson, Thomas Dance, Gregory Robinson, William Ricks, John Terry, Daniel McLoud and Robert Tuck.[3]

None of us now know much about them, just that they didn't end up as tulip bulbs on the beach, but were gathered up and carried onwards into the world.

For many years, there was a rumour of treasure that had gone down with the ships of the line. The wrecks were dived many times, but it wasn't until the 1980s that they really started bringing things up. What they found was displayed in Thorsminde, and over the years this grew into a museum to the *St George* and the *Defence*: the *St George* Shipwreck Museum, whose finest exhibit is the 38-foot rudder of the *St George*. It was found on the bar south of Lolland, where it had been lost before its fateful Christmas journey. In a new millennium, it was plucked out of oblivion and transported to Thorsminde, where a tower was later built so that visitors could wander from floor to floor and take it in: this giant, one Christmas night.

When I visited the beautiful shipwreck museum,[4] I wandered around the museum shop and café afterwards. Inside hung a series of photographs of a cutter in distress at sea. The series had been taken some time in the 1990s by the photographer Jørgen Borg. He had captured the locals as they stood peering out of the entrance to the harbour. Out at sea, a cutter was lying the way a cutter should not lie, and around it was the wall of water. I studied the series closely and afterwards had a cup of coffee with the museum's curator, Helle. We chatted about the handsome museum, the figureheads, the tulips at the bottom of my garden and the surfeit of international history that has washed up on the coast. We discussed the incomprehensible dimensions of the British ships of the line, and then I mentioned the photographs of the comparatively modest cutter in distress. I had been touched by the sight of the locals in the pictures. They were sheltering behind one another, or wherever else shelter was possible. The men with their binoculars, their eyes fixed on the cutter, which might not manage the storm.

'They're looking very intently at the ship out there,' I said. 'I wonder how the people out there are looking at the people ashore.'

Helle, glancing over at the ticket desk, said, 'It was Betina's husband out there. It was your husband's cutter, wasn't it, Betina?'

And a woman stuck her head out from behind the rack of postcards, and said:

'Yup.'

'That was your husband?' I asked in a quiet voice. Everything had ceased to be theory and adventure, and was now the fate of a family.

'Yes, that was him,' replied the woman.

'And he got through it?' I asked.

'Oh sure,' she said, and retreated back to her work, because there was probably nothing else to say, I suppose.

He got through it. Uncertainty is an everyday thing with a fisherman in the family, and the rest we can leave to the tombstones: 'In my distress I called upon the Lord, and cried unto my God.' Sometimes God listens, other times you have to crawl ashore yourself. Into the story and back out of it again. Nameless or beloved. At some vulnerable place, lifted in an instant out of the reality we know and into the next.

Winter
Solstice

Early morning, not long before Christmas. I'm taking the ferry across the Limfjord at Thyborøn. I'm going to Agger on the other side and further up the Danish coast. Light hangs in threads across the water. A little while ago, the ferry arrived. Cars disembarked. But there's half an hour until the next departure, so now we have to wait. That's all right. Sooner or later the ferry will leave, because a ferry has been leaving here as long as anyone can remember. A little black one we used to watch through binoculars from the Secret Place. There's a new ferry now, a new ferry terminal, but it's an old year. My grandmother once claimed to have driven straight across the water. They'd been on a senior citizens' excursion to Thy, just across the channel from Thyborøn. The bus driver went right over, she insisted. At the suggestion that this could not be true—it's at least half a mile of water—she merely snorted. We showed her a map, but she snorted at that too.

'If I say I drove to Thy, I drove to Thy,' she said.

She was probably keeping half the bus entertained. The person in charge of entertainment can't also keep an eye on the ferry service.

On the other side of the channel is the Agger Peninsula, and next the town of Agger itself. Around these windswept positions grew Thy, a region whose unmistakable beauty is reflected in its tiny name. The first time Thy was ever written down was in 1075, and it was spelt *Thiut*. Like the bright chirrup of a bird, like lark song, perhaps, and it makes it no less beautiful to know that *thiuth* apparently meant 'people'.

I have sailed across to those people often, and it's a good thing you can still take the ferry. How else could you experience the great tug of the channel? Over time, the inland waters were closed off to the sea by a thin strip of sand. That's why the Limfjord is called a fjord. But every now and then, the spit of sand was broken by a nasty storm, opening up a passage to the North Sea. The Vikings could slip out into the world that way. Small crafts, shipmasters, fishermen. The channel as it exists today, broad and sucking, appeared after a storm surge in 1862, and it's quite something. The ferry rocks violently halfway across if the tidal currents are going in or out. In the summertime, tourists in sandals lurch squealing around on deck. They haven't seen it coming, the pull. But judging by the queue, today it's only locals and long-distance drivers. We'll stay sitting in our vehicles on the way over. We know: the fjord arches its back out there. A river is embedded in the water's inner nature, and if we got out of our cars, we would hold firmly on to the railing, we would find a foothold. Somewhere to the south: my grandmother on the bus, shooting through the waves, over the herds of seals, back into the current, and I would wave to her, but today she's long since dead.

I'm waiting here. And waiting here is good: no motorway in the world can do for the soul what the ferry can, and there are days when time is exactly what you need. Days when time is sacred, and today is one such day. I'm sitting in my Toyota on the verge of deep winter. Of Christmas. Of cold. I'm not good at Christmas, and every year I consider travelling away from it, but you can't escape Christmas in Thy. The grey light drifts. At some point between the night that's coming and the day that dawns, the sun can't get any further down. Then it turns: at the solstice, where the sun stands still. It's an imperceptible moment that occurs while asleep, and I have a headache, I'm longing to sleep, but now there's movement on the ferry. Now the cars are starting up in the queue. Then the man in the boiler suit waves me forwards.

⚓

From the ferry, I drive straight to Thy National Park, or Cold Hawaii, as the coastline is also known these days. The national park as well as the surfers' paradise of Cold Hawaii start at the southern tip of the supernaturally beautiful Agger Peninsula. The edge of Cold Hawaii is currently drawn just north of Hanstholm Harbour, but let's face it: Cold Hawaii migrates like its name across borders, and as a surfing phenomenon these finned people have left traces far up and far down the coastline. Surfing culture has brought youth and higher education to the coast. Environmentalism, cargo bikes, skateboards, pregnancies and the world. They have beautiful bodies, salt in their hair, and were I still young

I'd fall in love with each and every one of them. But this is middle age, it's coming on Christmas, and I'm driving slowly up the peninsula. No need to rush along the stretch between the channel and Hanstholm. It's the best cruising route in the country:

Let the day turn, let the car sail. Feel your freedom, if you have it. Raise yourself above the unsolved riddles and sink into your seat. Meet the landscape like a bullet through flesh. Penetrate. There's only one road to follow here, my friend. It leads from you up into Thy, where realizations await. If you have a voice, sing now. You are alone. Sing! Let the darkness recede, the space atomize. You are with all the wildfowl that stand still. You're in Thy now, so sail in it.

In the summer, the cows wander across the salt meadows: lazy wildebeest. Now there are swans, geese, ducks. Somewhere along the road between here and Hanstholm, with or without binoculars, it will be possible to observe small flocks of camper vans, old VW microbuses and pickups. People in black wetsuits, like cormorants in the cold, gently bobbing in the breakers. The gulls always on the lookout for a fish. The surfers always on the lookout for a wave. The place they gather is the place where conditions that day are the best. But I see none of them on the peninsula today. I get lost in the swans. They're waiting, the fatty down against their bodies, for a slight tick in the tilt of the Earth. I wish my soul were as padded as theirs. It isn't, so I take the turning into town, buy a Christmas bun and a packet of paracetamol.

I keep driving north towards Lodbjerg Lighthouse. I want to go up the tower. That's what I want, yes, and it's been lashing with rain all autumn. The drainage pipes have given in. The streams are running over: the brooks can't show any moderation, as my grandmother would have said. Not knowing when enough is enough is a terrible trait, but even the puddles have upgraded to inland waters. This autumn's eternal rain is full of suspense; the water is rising in the strangest places. My Toyota is driving towards the lighthouse like grandma's bus, across some newly emerged wetlands. It should have been a jeep, but the lighthouse is as it should be.

From the towertop the view is grey, with the sea and the fjord on the periphery. The sky looks like dirty mop-water. It needs a light to come ashore and make it three-dimensional. Around the lighthouse is a forest. They planted trees on the dunes many decades ago to stop the sand encroaching on the villages, and now vast areas up and down the coast are covered in woodland. They were planted according to rules, but are full of surprises and mercy. To the sailors and fishermen, the storms posed the threat. To the rural population and the peasants in the hinterland, it was the shifting sands that were the worst. The more they farmed, the sandier they got. The more wars, the more fleets, the more wood was felled. A network of roots is like connective tissue beneath the skin. It holds everything firm and together. Like the fatty down against the birds' bodies.

Eventually, they realized that it was the roots holding the land firm. So they planted in the dunes. Here, there and everywhere along the coast. Where I live, there were trees planted at Husby. Further south there are Blåbjerg, Kærgård, Vrøgum, Vejers, Oksby and Ål. Here, high up on

Thy, the areas of woodland are called Lodbjerg, Hvidbjerg, Stenbjerg, Torup, Nystrup, Vilsbøl, Tved, Hjardemål and Lild: and so each local community has bound the dunes in place with trees and names. When the great woods below me have accomplished their primary task, they can be the other things they also are: spaces for rest and beauty. The red deer among the trees and in the wide clearings, the herds gigantic with does at the head. I feel like going down to them, like holding the trees. They whisper about the motion of the wind at the top; they have time for us.

I hike through the woods. The bone-white roots are pushing underneath the path, and the pine cones others would collect, I leave. It smells of moss and darkness here. One time, way up the coast by Jammerbugten—Misery Bay—a boy walked off and left his mother. He was three years old and wanted to take off his coat. Again and again, he took off the coat, and it was cold. So his mother put it on the wrong way round. It was an act of love, but it made him angry, and he left. Yes, he walked into the woods with the zip down his back. He walked purposefully through the dry late-winter grass and vanished underneath the heavy skirts of the tall spruces. He let the darkness descend. He wandered unhesitating, first in anger then in bewilderment. For, now, his mother was the one lost. Now it was she who had gone, and the night was alive with helicopters, baying dogs and tabloid journalists. A little boy like that can't help but die if he gets lost in woods as large as those. They reported on it minute by minute. There was breaking news for every siren that night, and by morning they were dragging the lakes in the heart of the forest. Men in wetsuits, parents crumbling with grief and worry, hardened police chiefs with shaky hands, and then a man came riding up on an Iceland pony. He often goes riding in the woods, peering in through the tree trunks. And there he meets a strange sight. A child among the spruce needles. Runny-nosed, pale-faced and trembling. It's light now, and the child has walked through the night with the zipper down his back.

No one can know, because a boy of three has no words to describe it. But I imagine him walking till the dark became its own being. He nestled into it. In the depths of the dark, there is either what you fear to find, or what you only dream of. I picture him coming across an aeroplane in the core of the forest, abandoned in a clearing by a German soldier, or maybe an Allied soldier but the boy has no concept of the enemy. The cockpit is open, the wings are streamlined, and he clambers up into the plane. He settles in front of the control stick. Mouth open, nose running; but the coat is zipped and warm. And then the plane rises in a dream above the forest, and the little boy with moss on his knees glides a curving swoop above his fate. There it is, down there, in a flicker of sweeping searchlights. He can see the cars' red tail lights, like glittering eyes in all that black. There are blue flashes, and orange. That's the fear running rampage down there, but he can see the sea, the boy with the zipper, he sees the stars, and in the east is the distant glow of the coming light. He shuts his eyes, lets himself be carried, and lands in the moss, vanishing into sleep until the water has been sucked up through his trousers. Then he stretches, then he gets to his feet and wanders out of the darkness, into the forest of firs, nearing the man with the horse.

Back in the car, I put the heating on by my feet. They're playing Handel's *Messiah* on the radio. 'Lift up thy voice with strength,' they sing, and there it is again, Thy.[1] 'Lift up thy voice with strength; lift it up, be not afraid,' they sing as I drive around the national park with paracetamol, a Christmas bun and a Thermos of coffee. At least I remembered the coffee this morning, I think, turning off towards a small church. My intention was to eat my bun in the car park and wash down a couple of pills with the coffee, but it's so small, the church, that I have to fish out the map. This is Lodbjerg Church, it turns out, and sometimes, when your faith in forests is greater than your faith in Christmas, it's good to enter into these places.

The church is steeple-less, the windows carefully painted, and there's a bench overlooking the view. Someone's looking after the place, I realize, as I cross the gravel. It's neatly raked, all the graves are decorated for Christmas, and it's warm inside the church.

You can take in everything all at once in here. The low wooden ceiling, paved floor and small box pews for the parish souls. The remains of two frescoes by the chancel arch. One depicts a large snake, the other the Virgin Mary with the Infant Jesus in her arms. Large as life, she's painted, and I sit down in a pew in front of her.

I close my eyes a moment. I could sleep, but last time I was in Thy, it was midsummer. I drove down along the coast from the north, moving along the big garlands the coastline makes from Misery Bay via Vigsø Bay to the city of Hanstholm. I was looking forward to cruising through the wildlife reserve. It's an incomprehensibly epic landscape for such a tiny country, but when I got to Hjardemål Church I stopped to use the toilet. Afterwards I tried the door to the church, but that one was locked. Once bitten, I thought, sitting down in a patch of sun on the grass, for the year I was born, in late summer, a group of hippies occupied the church. They had artistic aspirations, political manifestos and chemically altered brains. Lying under a tarp, they played guitar all summer in Jutland's answer to Christiania, the infamous commune in Copenhagen: Camp Frøstrup, Camp Thy, the New Society—the newcomers had many names. They whipped up an atmosphere, eager to make political art and light a bit of a fire under those arsehole reactionaries. And so they reconnoitred the area, looking for a church they could occupy. They chose Hjardemål, and they gained access at night. By morning there were banners hanging from the steeple, and the action was supposed to last a week. That was not what happened, for now they had kicked down the door to God's house, and to rage. They had been tolerated long enough, the locals thought. Enough was enough, and word went round the fishermen at Hanstholm Harbour. They came swiftly, with their bike chains and fishing gear as weapons. Others turned up with cudgels, leather straps and canvas slappers. A crowd gathered around the church. You'd have thought it was a confirmation, but Camp they were curious. I was invited for coffee and tea. There I was, apparently role-less, talking about my work and my family's ties with the coast. As though both were a ticket into the community.

But I was difficult to integrate. In any case, there was the risk that a husbandless woman like me might run off with another woman's man. And other women's men saw me and thought: an outsider like her, coming here without a husband and kids, is a sorry sight. Or is she a rebel? Yes, she must be a rebel. Rebels are a threat to the prevailing order.

I started drinking coffee with the women whose children had flown the nest, and whose husbands had gradually run to seed. Except that they woke up, the husbands, when I came. For, yes, I was indeed a sorry excuse for a woman—or rather, I was a free woman, and a free woman might give the wife ideas. So he would sit there, the husband, wanting to dominate the coffee table. The stray had to be dealt with.

In the end, I discovered that the places I could be most myself were with the neighbours who saw me as a human being, and with the widows. With widows, there was no longer any order to uphold, and so there was room for me. Tove Ditlevsen, one of the most ground-breaking authors in Danish literature, once said of her existential childhood dreams: I wanted to be a widow and I wanted to be a poet,[3] and she was right about that, because there I was, harmless among the bereaved, and writing, writing. And when I wasn't sitting there, I drove up and down the coast to meet the landscape's other strays. And I travelled to distant countries, deeply rooted yet perpetually on my journey.

But the Cold Hawaiians' fate has not been that. Like the hippies, they, too, were outsiders coming to Thy. They poured their love into the fishing village of Klitmøller, south of Hanstholm, towards the end of the 1970s. In those days, the village was much like all the others along the coast. A bit of boat-fishing off the beach. Old fogeys in blue Kansas boiler suits, wives with root perms and ravaged smiles. Here and there a couple of restless youths on Puch Maxis. Everything faintly dying and winding down, as places do when there's no future for the young, no jobs to be had and everything persists in the backwards-looking resolve that things cannot change. For a couple of centuries, Klitmøller—a harbour for small vessels, known as a *skudehavn*—had thrived. In the seventeenth century, it traded with Norway, which lay just on the other side of the sea. Back then the Limfjord wasn't open to the sea, so goods were transported into the country through Klitmøller. The settlement, in its exposed location, flourished as a waystation. Then, in 1825, the sea broke through to the Limfjord down near Agger. Norwegian cargo ships could sail east now, so the village had to scratch a living off fishing alone, which they did until the late 1960s. Then the fishing moved north, to the splendid new harbour at Hanstholm, home to Bent Ironbar. Klitmøller began to lose its lifeblood. Plywood boards appeared at the windows; but then they came: the surfers.

The locals didn't like them much. They'd not had good experiences with outsiders who came in large groups. Just look at Hjardemål Church and Camp Thy, to say nothing of the Nazis, who had built the biggest fortification in Scandinavia at Hanstholm. Festung Hanstholm, the

Germans called the place. It was meant to be 'Scandinavia's Gibraltar', and they arrived with cement mixers, heavy artillery, radars, thousands of soldiers, casual labourers and prisoners of war.[4] They built, wreaked havoc and test-fired the artillery, and before long the local population had to abandon house and home. In an act of collaborationism, it was the Danish state who helped its own citizens evacuate. You don't forget that sort of thing, and I read somewhere that a few people bluntly called the surfers pigs in the beginning. The war was still under their skin. It takes time for deep wounds to heal. But more and more of the surfers came. They came with different customs, a different view of nature, a different kind of materialism. They came from the big cities, including ones abroad, and they were not tourists. Tourists the locals were used to. They came and went, they were funny to look at, but they had money in their pockets. The surfers lived in camper vans, if they hadn't simply moved into the little fishing village. They bought houses, and in numbers that took the plywood out of the windows.

Yet there was, they discovered, something to be gained from the surfers. They were skilled, hardworking, young and athletic. They brought women with them, they provided fertile ground for nurseries and trade. They changed conditions on the coast and the assortment of goods available at the grocer's for the better. They cooperated, and today men like Bent Ironbar have grandchildren who surf, teach others to surf, own surfing shops, or study in Aalborg, Aarhus or Copenhagen while he or she longs to return to Thy, where the waves are better than anywhere else.

Because they are better here, the waves. Storms between Scotland and Norway send swells down towards Denmark, and they hit slap bang between Agger and Hanstholm, right where the coast forms an angle of nearly ninety degrees. It creates several ideal surf spots. The most famous of these are Fakir, Klitmøller Reef and the Middles, where I saw them last summer, and there are plenty of other spots with exotic names up and down the coast. They cross borders, the Cold Hawaiians, but they don't occupy churches, and they have become a lifeblood here. A kind of hope that vibrates underneath everything in—and beyond—Thy; and in a little while I'll be driving up to where they are, I think, sitting on the pew opposite the Virgin Mary.

Did I doze off? Yes, I might have, but I'm about to drive further north, now, to a landing place where the Cold Hawaiians are often to be found, looking sexy in the breakers. They eat lunch at the North Sea Café, with sand in their hair and cheeks flushed. They drink Thy Pilsner with the other locals, and I want to sit there and be in the same room as them. While they lick beer off the bottle, my eyes will lick salt off them, and once I've done that I'll cruise on further north. Oh yes, I want to cruise through Thy. To sail north in my Toyota through the wildlife reserve. To let its grandeur raise me to a high summit in my mind, exploding time; yes, exploding it into atoms. That's the sort of thing you're capable of, Thy. You are wilder than most: blast the Christmas trees, the peeling small towns' creaky lamp-post decorations, blast them all to hell. I want to drive right through you with something harsh on the sound system. Until I see Hanstholm Lighthouse on its promontory. Right into the very core of darkness, that's where I want to go, and then I'll stop. Let it all meld into one. Nuzzle into Thy like a roaming wolf. Shut my eyes, open them, and look—there's Mary, holding the zipped-up boy in her arms.

And I feel something on my face. Or I realize that when I shut my eyes before, it was because the sunlight was bothering me. It's falling through the church window by the pulpit. I didn't realize the weather had cleared. But it must have done, I think, turning my face to the light. I sit for a while, rise from the pew, and go outside to take a closer look.

It has indeed: the sun has risen above Thy like a glaring searchlight. It hangs low, as it should, ready for the picking. Somewhere to the south-east, the light is reflected in a lake, and sparkles. I stand quietly outside the door, listening. 'Thiut, thiut,' comes the sound of a winter bird in the undergrowth, and there is wind in the treetops; there is a tick in the tilt of the Earth and feet on the gravel. A woman steps out around the corner of the apse. She's in overalls and has her hat pulled down around her ears. She smiles at me and heads towards the porch.

'I see the light's come,' she says as she walks past me.

'Yes, it's come,' I say, but she has gone.

Magnets

W e don't know how birds find their way. Not really. We just know that every year they fly in their millions along the East Atlantic migration route. They fly as winter approaches, from the Arctic tundra in Canada, Greenland and Siberia down along the line of the west coast of Europe, which is now called the East Atlantic Flyway. And as summer approaches, they head north again. Even the smallest birds can fly up to 10,000 miles. First to get somewhere warm and to eat, next to reach the cool Arctic summer to breed. Some say they use the sun and stars as landmarks, like the human navigators of the past. Others believe they have a biological clock that can compensate for the turning of the universe. But how does a little wading bird know the universe is turning? If my mother hadn't pointed to the Great Bear and taught me to follow its travels, would I have known?

The birds remember the landscape far below them. As though the landscape were a readable language, and the transition between sea and mainland a drawn stroke that to the birds five miles above looks like a route. And it is one. But coastlines, lakes, stretches of road change. Landmarks come and go. People are always hoarding things. The sea takes back what it can. And we still don't know how the birds navigate. Even tiny, newly hatched chicks on the tundra can find Africa. Blind birds can find their way.

Researchers think that birds have a sensory organ in their eyes. This organ is a barometer capable of measuring even minute changes in pressure. A storm can mean drowning for a small migratory bird. The bird knows this. It knows something I need to find out. Or simply something I've forgotten, perhaps, because I have lived in windproof houses, sat at screens, switched on the radio, opened the fridge, slept in mass-produced pyjamas flown in by planes with radar systems. Not that humanity isn't capable: my car has GPS.

Some birds use their sense of smell to navigate, and I have seen the waders' long bills, the way they bend, double over, and operate in sandy beds like sewing needles. It's hard to get your head round how a bill like that can register the scents of the savannah, the Rhine delta, of Svalbard, so far above the Earth. Humans only smell what's on us at that altitude, but birds are planes of blood, bone, feathers and stamina, and in their eyes, where the barometer is, there is a molecular compass too. This is how the bird orients itself, by using the Earth's magnetic field: inside your ears, if you're a migratory bird, are small hair cells containing a magnetic substance. Your senses are alert; you have hatched into the quivering needle of a compass.

On the collar beam in my childhood home (until the Roads Authority razed it to the ground), we had one such compass needle. It took the shape of a stuffed common snipe. My dad had caught it, as he put it. When I asked him if he'd shot it, he said, 'Yes, I caught it—think it was at Rind Stream.'

It watched with eyes of glass as our daily lives unfolded below. Its bill pointed us out, while its body, stuffed with chemicals and kapok, had been shaped into a pose that said 'running briskly across a meadow'.

I assume my dad shot it, but I prefer the word 'caught' as well. That word brings my father's hands before my eyes. He has only seven fingers, because as a young carpenter and new dad he had a run-in with a milling machine. Was he trying to catch the machine too? His left hand is a stump with a stitched-on index finger. A person who catches birds doesn't want to kill; he only wants to take a closer look. The little navigator isn't afraid of the world: it was created to exist in it. Yet in its captured state, its essence dies, and then it died between my father's seven fingers. It let the white membranes of its eyes roll up. Vanishing. Until its resurrection on the collar beam, now stitched back together. There it stood, gazing down at us with inscrutable affection.

It could navigate, and so could the living members of its species. There's a beauty to our not knowing how, and yet some things we do know. We know that migratory birds fly for days without rest, food or sleep, losing more than half their body weight. They can't keep going indefinitely, so they make pit stops where there's food and convenient places to rest. One such spot is the Wadden Sea. Out on the vast tidal flats, which stretch from the Skallingen Peninsula in the north through the marshland of Southern Jutland, across the border into Germany, into all the sandy, clay-slick crannies between the Frisian islands, and as far as Den Helder in Holland, the wetlands teem with life. Because of the Earth's rotation, there are six hours and twelve minutes between low tide and high tide. The water brings sand and clay with it. Plants cling hard to the flats. There is growth, a density of nutrients, life. The birds gather in ever-greater clusters inshore as the water rises, little by little, and eventually there are huge flocks of them standing on one leg, their bills under their wings. They are tired after their long journey; they sleep. Be still, now.

Like nomads, they lead a simple life. They breed on the tundra because there's plenty of space between neighbours, less risk of infection spreading, and the harsh northern winters reduce the number of predators. The birds can sit on their makeshift nests and focus on parenting. They pluck the feathers from their breasts. They want to reach the bare skin. That's where it's warmest, and once the skin is bare, the bird folds its breast over the eggs. It gives them its warmth, hatches its young, watches their long legs strut among the crowberry stalks. The bird has faith. It knows its downy children are born with a sense of direction. In autumn, the journey will take them south. As it travels, the baby bird will move through a vast space. It sews stitches in the Earth with its bill. Changes its plumage, flies in formation; it doesn't flaunt the nine air sacs stowed away between its organs. They branch into its bones and function like bellows. They carry oxygen for the journey along the East Atlantic migration route, lifting the bird across borders, helping it make full use of its senses, while its wings carry it far away into the world.[1]

188

It's magical. It's greater than we can understand, and in the town of Vester Vedsted, not far from Denmark's southern border, a place has been built to honour what we know and what we don't. They call the building the Wadden Sea Centre and have wrapped it in reeds.[2] The building emerges out of the soil to kiss the landscape of which it is part. Inside, I understood a little more. I spent ages walking around. As the light shifted in the rooms, it felt as though my layers of protection disappeared. My skin turned to newly frozen water, easily splintered, penetrated. You've got to pluck the feathers from your breast to imbue as much life into the work as possible, I thought. Gingerly, I stroked the brickwork. Sat for ages over coffee in the café, readying myself for the world again. The Wadden Sea Centre is the first building I've ever laid my cheek against as I left. We don't understand all these things, and yet they exist, I thought, as I nestled into it. The birds find their way—even the blind ones.

I found my way to the Wadden Sea myself, driving, but first I stopped short in my wellies and stared at the tractor-drawn buses you can take to the nearby island of Mandø. The buses weren't running in the chronic rain. In the museum shop, they'd said I shouldn't plan on reaching the island without a snorkel. March, and it's been such a wet winter. The wind wasn't helping. Mandø lay in relative isolation at the end of access roads now submerged by the tide.

When I lived by the Wadden Sea, I'd often stand on the southern tip of Fanø and gaze across at Mandø. You could see it clearly to the south-east. Droves of birds frolicking around out there. The route to the island is nearly always open by air. At the time, I thought about the surprises in store for you if you imagined you could walk there from the southern tip of Fanø, which is the next island up. Occasionally it looked like the trek might be doable. God knows how many people, prompted by ignorance or overconfidence, have made an attempt over the years, I thought. What tideways, deeps and trenches had they found out there? One moment they're strolling across the flats, then a few hours later they're up to their necks in water, or trapped on a sandbar with a seal.

One day, I had decided, I wanted to visit the island by tractor-drawn bus, but in Vester Vedsted these many years later, the buses were empty and locked. A flock of greylag geese passed in V-formation above me and my raincoat.

'There's a human down there,' they said. 'It's got no wings,' they said.

But I did have wheels, so I entered the address of a rented cabin on the Wadden Sea island of Rømø. For the most part, you don't get much benefit from GPS in the Wadden Sea. Out there, you need to have faith in the innate ability of homo sapiens to find your way around. If you can rely on this ability in a psychological space. For the Wadden Sea is, in many ways, a piece of psychology. The year I lived in the middle of it, I was fascinated by how it affected me and the people I met in the area. I was doing a residency—in other words, another kind of nomad. But the newcomers who had taken up permanent residence in the Wadden Sea had to find a way to live with that vast image in the mind's eye. It was my impression that some of them had chosen the place because they were dependent on the horizon, and did not thrive on being trapped among too many constricting buildings. For them, the Wadden Sea was visual calm, oxygen in their lungs, and a sense of time that expanded and brought peace of mind. More often than not they were to be found in a kind of conversation with the birds, the animals, the silence, and thrived. Another group, it seemed to me, had decided to move to the Wadden Sea because they dreamt of a cleaner, more authentic life. They were the first to leap into regional dress, and thus often the subject of local gossip. For others, it was the urge to make time stand still with hollyhocks, timber frames and romance. These utopian notions often started by building the door through which evil can enter. It would take time to get the devil in hand, as it slunk around as it pleased and destroyed the idyll. Then there were those who used the Wadden Sea as a kind of shelter against the temptations and menace of the big city. A place that, judging by its position at the extreme west of the map, had got to be sufficiently far away from alcohol, drugs and violence. A vacuum.

But a vacuum is always waiting to be filled with something. In the Wadden Sea, you bring the contents with you, and the contents of a supposedly authentic life can be terrifying. Relief found those who sought it, and so the clink of bottles in plastic bags from the grocer's became a sound that felt almost as local to me as the chatting birds on their way across the flats.

'There's a powerful thirst in people here,' a native once said to me. The natives lived with the landscape as though it were a part of them. Where one began and the other ended was hard to say. But it was my pet theory that this thirst came with the Wadden Sea and the culture of the islands, and for some it also came with the things we deposit in both. The place was supposed to improve your life, but it simply trapped you in the life you already had, only now without a filter: your demons came with you. Without the constant opportunity afforded by the city to give your demons the slip down a side street, to distract them with consumption and entertainment, to take your focus off them in the crowd, you're mercilessly stuck with them. You're naked here, exposed, deprived of your protective layers. There are no feathers on your breast.

During my time at the residency on Fanø, I was visited once by a colleague from Copenhagen. Back then I didn't have a driving licence, so we'd agreed to meet at the station in Ribe. Ribe is beautiful, ancient, snug, and the colleague, who wrote poems, loved every single cobble, every nook. She wasn't even cowed by a walk up the spectacularly medieval Commoners' Tower of the cathedral, which overlooks the painfully flat landscape. We could see Ribe from up there too, of course. But as we approached Esbjerg by train, sailed across to Fanø and took the virtually empty Sønderho bus south, I sensed a psychological depression forming beside me.

'Doesn't it get quite dark here in the evening?' she said.

'It's fine,' I said. 'I like that it's a bit gritty.'

But it was new to her, so she spent the next few days wandering around, getting to grips with the rising and

falling developing agent of the landscape. Sønderho itself
was reassuring. More than anything else the village looked
like an open-air museum, but you didn't have to walk far
before there it was again: the vacuum. It lurked around
every corner.

In the end, we spent most of our time at the Poet's Place,
the retreat where I was living. Now with a slightly dripping box of red wine and, for my part, a certain steadily
increasing irritation. Her poems were good. But a person
who writes can't opt out of a phenomenon like the Wadden
Sea, I told myself. It wants something with you, that thing
out there, and it doesn't owe you or the reader cosiness, I
concluded, sitting there under the shipmaster's low ceilings.

It might have been because of this that I decided to tell
my colleague that people said there was a kind of Bermuda
Triangle out there in the Wadden Sea. If you drew a line
from the southern tip of Fanø to Ribe Cathedral, then down
to the northern end of Rømø and back, it formed a triangle.
In the middle of this triangle is the strange tidal island of
Mandø. At that exact spot, I told her, people would go
missing without trace. While the Bermuda Triangle of the
North Atlantic transformed huge vessels into ghost ships,
wiping them and any planes that might be passing off the
radar—aided by either paranormal energy or the massive,
hundred-foot waves that can arise so rapidly in the area
between Bermuda, Florida and the Greater Antilles—the
Wadden Sea Triangle was more subtle. The fact was, however, I told the poet, that people seemed to be drawn to
Mandø. And they went missing. A son might say that, in the
days leading up to his disappearance, his father had been

talking urgently about that specific island. He'd kept telling his son that it was 'singing'. Another had scribbled down enough signs and omens to make Nostradamus jealous.

'Vulnerable people often see omens,' I said to the poet.

She nodded, and I told her about the woman with the porcelain dogs. The woman, up until the time she disappeared, had been saying to the neighbours that she was considering moving to Mandø. But there are around thirty-five souls on the island, and it's not the kind of place where there's always room for one more, so the neighbours shrugged it off. But then she vanished; and from the age of shipmasters onwards, it's been traditional to keep a pair of porcelain dogs in your windows. They're meant to signal whether the man of the house is away sailing or at home. If they're facing outwards, he's at sea; inwards, and he's at home. When they forced their way into the woman's house—her sister was getting worried because she wasn't picking up the phone—they found them, the porcelain dogs. They were everywhere. The woman had been buying and collecting porcelain dogs the same way some women start collecting dolls. No human being entering the home of a doll collector can re-emerge without lasting damage to the soul, and when they reached the bed, they found the soft impression of a body that had slept there. The duvet was cast aside, but her slippers were no longer in their usual place. She was like a sleepwalker who had walked so far into sleep that she had left with it.

'Jesus,' said my guest.

'Poof, gone,' I said, as the boxed wine dripped from the table onto the linoleum flooring in the kitchen. 'Never seen since. No body found. Not here, not in Germany, not England-way. The deeps out there can suck down a little of everything.'

After that we needed another glass. We talked about the Bermuda Triangle. About waves a hundred feet tall, and how high that was in comparison to the flagpole at the Poet's Place. Afterwards she wanted to go to bed, but I could hear her talking on the phone to someone for ages, and I felt guilty. It was just something I'd made up. There was no factual truth to the story, apart from the stuff about putting porcelain dogs in the window. And about signs and omens. At breakfast, the poet said she'd barely slept. It turned out she'd been a bit of a sleepwalker as a child. One time they'd found her on the street in Copenhagen in her nightie.

'If sleep can lure a child out of an apartment, down the stairs and out the front door, what could it tempt a sleeping adult into doing here?' she said.

'It was just a story,' I said.

'But I can feel something out there,' she said.

I don't think I ever suggested to her that what she could sense out there was probably her demons. Nothing else, unless you believed it was God. But we didn't talk about demons or God. We drank red wine, and she went home a day early. Something to do with her boyfriend, she said. But on the way to the bus she shot anxious glances at the dogs in the windows.

You've got to be careful with the stories you tell other people. I remembered that as I got into my car at Vester Vedsted. And you've got to be careful what stories you tell yourself, I noted, driving away from the stranded tractor-drawn buses. I set off for the coast, and from there across the long causeway to Rømø. There's something practical, patient and generous about this causeway. It's been knocked through by storm surges several times, but it makes the horizon-dependent eye happy as it crosses. Seen in aerial photographs, the road through the North Sea, over five miles long, looks like an umbilical cord, supplying nourishment to Rømø in the role of the foetus. The island's wide west-facing sandy beaches: the backbone. The green, east-facing marshy coast: the soft organs. I drove slowly out towards the island. The marsh was wet with rain, although the windscreen wipers had stopped. Finally a break in the weather, I thought, turning south at the end of the causeway. I wanted a walk around the flats before I found my rented cabin, and before long there it was: Sønderstrand Beach, out of season. No kite buggies, no land sailing. To the north: the squelching sandy bed and then the mountainous dunes, protruding like distant and enormous camels. To the south, something that looked like a glutinous and endless desert, and then the ships from the nearby towns of Havneby and List, pressing onwards somewhere on the indefinable periphery.

The wind was in the east. Down around my boots, the water was being sucked out of the landscape. I walked in a vaguely southerly direction. The first half hour I kept an eye on the other hikers. After that, the landscape had me in its grip. I peered at tidal grooves, odd graphic designs in the layer of silt, looked for amber, ran into a little flock of sandpipers, peed, and enjoyed watching the moon, which was waxing, draw the urine off towards Lister Deep. I met a seal. We accompanied each other south, me in the sand, it in the water. I told it that its being and my being were essentially the same. I told it: 'We are of the same essence,' and I promised it I'd never dream of trying to catch it. Then it squelched down into the trench it had found off the Wadden Sea's strange, virginal breakers. I squinted, looking for Esbjerg Power Station's chimney, and Mandø. At one point I quoted a poem I'd forgotten I knew by heart. Out loud. I sang. Out loud. And then I remembered the snipe. The one emptied of its internal magnets, which stood on the collar beam and pointed affectionately down at us. A delicate creature from a special region, and a beautiful and sad memorial to something that, like the bulldozed childhood home, had long since disappeared. I remembered it suddenly and clearly. I remembered the word 'caught'; I sensed the lighting in a room that no longer exists. I lost my layers of protection. I felt grief for the losses that have been and the losses to come. I turned the dogs in random directions, wishing I could hold time still, like my father had held it in the snipe. But we can't stop time. We can't escape the force that draws us through the world. We have magnets in our bodies.

Borderland

It's the same moon. In my memory, it's hovering above the transformer substation in the divide between our place and the neighbour's farm. I often used to play with the neighbours' boy, Peter, and had to pass it on the way home. But the substation doesn't exist anymore; the divide no longer matters. It vanished with the expropriation of my parents' land. For a long time, the farmhouse was left with all the windows ripped out, emptied of its contents, exposed to the parish. Then the Roads Authority removed the whole thing and laid the new road. Now and again, I drive over the spot in my car, but everything is the wrong way round. South of the road is the farm where Peter's family lived. It's been bought by a pig farmer, but the apple trees still bear fruit. The deer, foxes, birds, mice and motorists who stop to take a piss eat the fruit. The order of our little world is gone. As though washed into the sea.

But it's the same moon as always, and what's gone still lives in me. I'm standing on top of a dune in Listland, on the island of Sylt in the Federal Republic of Germany. I'm absorbing the landscape's peculiar balance of the recognizable and the alien. It's utterly self-contained, this countryside. It does not speak Danish, Frisian, Southern Jutish or German. It speaks body language, it unfolds in memory, and it does as it pleases. The sun is setting in the west; the moon has risen, immense. The first stars are appearing above a colossal migrating dune to the east. I can't tell if I'm in Colorado, playing a part in a western, or if this is the world as the world looked before humanity shaped spears, made fire, formed clans, put up fences, called upon god, scratched boundaries and built towers to place on them. But I'm middle-aged, and the last ferry to Denmark leaves from List in an hour. I'm going home before nightfall, yet in my mind the moon is hanging over the substation. I'm on my way home from Peter's. At his house, there are pictures of Jesus in black-varnished frames. In one of them, he's wandering through a desert of inconceivable dimensions, clad in a pink robe. At our house, we're members of the Church of Denmark, and that's it. But at Peter's, Jesus wears nice sandals. Jesus sandals. Only I can't call them that in front of Peter's dad. They were in fashion when I was a child, actually; people wore them. I wasn't allowed to swear at Peter's either. We did on our side of the divide. Yes, in my fatherland we swore.

It's May but cool, and I've got to make the ferry. It's been a clear day on the island with three names: Sild in Danish, Söl in North Frisian, Sylt in German. It doesn't care what we call it, and what it calls itself is none of our business. It has changed hands over time, but risen above it. This landscape is greater than lines in the sand. Always in the process of becoming, always dying and resurrecting, and I've been driving around the island all day long. The cliffs, the dunes and the sandy beaches are like the ones back home. The buildings remind me of the West Frisian styles I've seen on Rømø and Fanø, even as far down as Den Helder in Holland. The Frisians like houses with big thatched hats. They are broad-gabled, and the walls rear high above the front door. A walk through the village of Keitum and into the history museum there took me straight back to Johanne's house on Fanø. The tiles, the same. The treasured artefacts, the whaling and long voyages of the past, the same. The Frisian spirit has crossed the water in order to suffuse everything. And yet, all day, Sylt has seemed to me like a German island. Not just because of the language, but also the way of being in the landscape. You sit in numbered beach chairs with footrests, sheltered from the wind, on large terraces overlooking the beach. In Denmark, you'd sit on a blanket you'd brought with you and put up with the wind. But they don't stint on equipment in Germany, and certainly not on Sylt, which has been called the Federal Republic's answer to St-Tropez. And I can't put the difference into words any other way. Would I know I was in a foreign country if I hadn't written DON'T FORGET PASSPORT on my palm? Yes. I would know it the way I knew something had changed at the substation.

I have driven from north to south on Sylt. It's the biggest and northernmost of the German Wadden Sea islands, but still easy to get the lay of on a Saturday. In 1920, at the fateful referendum that drew the border based on national allegiance, it voted to join Germany. Its sister to the north, Rømø, went to Denmark. Now each belongs to its respective country, although as landscapes they are similar, and subject to the same ever-present threat of erosion and ruin.

When it comes to erosion, it's storm surges that are most dangerous. The earliest one on record is Saint Marcellus's flood in 1362, known in Danish as the Great Drowning of Men. A superstorm announced its arrival in January of that year. It caused the ice to crack into large pieces, which acted like battering rams against the dikes. Thousands of people and animals drowned, great tracts of land disappeared, and a number of the islands we know today were formed in a single night. South of Sylt—which during this storm surge, incidentally, lost its physical connection to the mainland and became a thin island in the Wadden Sea—the town of Rungholt vanished into the water. For many years, it was assumed that the tales of a Northern Atlantis called Rungholt were just that, tales. But mentions of Rungholt were later found in old documents, described as a flourishing merchant town. And between 1921 and 1938, the tides changed in such a way that remnants of embankments, buildings and wells suddenly began to materialize in the Wadden Sea. Based on these finds, it was estimated that the town had been relatively large. In addition to fragments of buildings, they found pottery, coins, gemstones, remnants of a ship from Crete and lapis lazuli from Afghanistan, not to mention an anchor from the Minoan era. A Northern Atlantis indeed, but difficult to excavate because of the tides, and anyway, you're not allowed to go digging up a World Heritage Site. The current theory about the city is that it had been a centre of coastal trade since ancient times, until one January night in 1362, when a single storm surge of climate-catastrophic dimensions washed it into the sea and altered the coastline.

Storm surges come and go. They're part of the organic, changeable and violent life of the coast, but from time to time one comes along that's worse than the rest. The All Saints' Day Flood, for instance. It swept an entire parish into the sea, and that same November night in 1436, the town of Ejdum on Sylt was engulfed in the waves as well. In the period after the most violent storm surges, people didn't dare live in the Wadden Sea at all for fear of drowning. They tried to keep to the *Geest*, the higher-lying areas of land within the marsh. But with each generation, important understanding falls away, and in 1634 people were settled once more on the fragile border between sea and land. One of these people was the Dutch engineer Jan Leeghwater. He lived in that year of our Lord on the German–Danish border, behind a small dike by the village of Dagebüll. He lived there with his son while working on a drainage project nearby. On the 10th of October he dropped in for a chat with the local carpenter, Pieter Jansz, but he hurried home to his boy when the wind picked up. As the evening wore on, the storm worsened and became a hurricane. Jan and his son went to bed with all their clothes on, but couldn't sleep for the noise. Later that night, the boy—Adriaan was his name—noticed something coming from the roof. 'There's saltwater dripping on my face, Father,' said the boy in the dark. It was the waves, which had clambered so far up the dike that sea spray was now raining down on the house. The storm roared in the ears of father and son. It was like the Lord himself screaming in their faces. Small foxes in the cave's sodden darkness; and then came a knock at the door. Warden Siewert had arrived, and he wanted them to come with him. It was now or never, and they ran through the storm. They ran with Siewert in an inferno of flying planks and boards. They were seeking shelter at the local manor house, and somewhere in the night Siewert shrieked that they needed a miracle. Miracle or not: they reached the manor. So did eighteen other residents of Dagebüll. They sat around the tallow candles and prayed for mercy to the god whose deluge was now upon them.

In his testimony after the disaster, Jan stated: 'I have been to the beach, where I have seen terrible things. Countless dead people and animals, as well as beams from houses, shattered carts, scores of trees, straw and rubbish.'[1]

Jan Leeghwater and his boy survived. It was a miracle. Pieter Jansz, the carpenter, and everyone in his household drowned, and they weren't the only ones. The storm surge of 1634, later called the Burchardi flood in English and in Danish the Second Great Drowning of Men, took between eight and fifteen thousand lives. On Nordstrand, then an island south-east of Sylt, the sea broke through forty-four dams. Six thousand out of nine thousand inhabitants drowned, and nineteen of the island's twenty-two churches were carried away.

It's always out there, the great storm surge. You know it's coming. The dikes grow and protect, but Sylt, which is thin around the waist, is in constant danger of snapping and breaking off into several islands. Geoscience and technology institutions around the world are researching the superstorms of the future and how to resist them. So

206

I must admit: I'm in love with the windswept character of the marshland, with the locks, with the sheep on the dikes, with the style of the buildings, with the watermills and windmills and what they call *værft*, mounds of earth the people heaped and built their farms on, safe from storm surges. They look like little castles, each with its own chatelaine. I love the language of South Jutland. Its connections to North Frisian, Low German, Dutch, and the way it breathes life and music into my own mother tongue—I love it. I love, too, how the word *værft* runs south through the marshland under similar names, like *wierde, woerd, warf, warft, werf, werve,* until early on it reaches the marsh around the Rhineland as *terp*.[2] It has crossed borders, this word, and my West Jutish grandparents used it too, when they heaped gravel, soil, dung. The latter—*mødding* in Danish—is still shovelled in Scotland in the form of midding and medding, for good words travel where they please. Water, too, respects no bounds. It takes what it wants when it wants it, and I have visited all the locks: Chamber Lock, Kongeå Lock, Ballum Lock, Vidå Lock, Højer Lock. I have seen the wooden columns, bolt upright, that mark how high the waters came during the Burchardi flood of 1634, during the Christmas flood of 1717, during the November storm of 1981, during the hurricane in 1999. I have seen the locks close, shutting out an accompanying river in the world with a large and beautiful brick-built gatehouse. I have walked along the dikes and imagined the watery hell on Earth that is a storm surge, but for me, the marsh is still like a paradise, where the eye can rest. Margrethe Polder, New Frederik's Polder, Old Frederik's Polder, land reclaimed

from the sea, are all true royalty. I admire the capacity here
for survival, the vaulted sky, the outlook, and the eternal
interchange of starlings, culture and people. Yet despite
my unconditional love, when I stay in the borderland, I'm
always afraid of saying the wrong thing. Not a word about
Jesus and his sandals. One time, I caught a lift to the station with a South Jutlander from the local college, where I
taught. I was getting a train to Copenhagen. As we crossed
the river Kongeå, I said:

'What's this little stream?'

I knew perfectly well it was the Kongeå! I knew perfectly
well it marked the border between Denmark and Germany
from 1864 to 1920. That it had severed families, lovers,
siblings, the course of lives. I knew it was the difference
between life and death to be on one side or the other of
that river, if you were a young man during the First World
War. I understood that it was a sacred river in Danish history, and I knew it was charged with sorrow and trauma,
but in my fatherland, we swear. We say silly things when
we mustn't, and the driver was angry.

Every time I cross the Kongeå or simply hear it mentioned, I feel ashamed, because this was a thing whose scope
I did not understand. The fact is, I don't see all the invisible
dividing lines in the borderland. They speak their allegiance
in code. The people I meet have traumas, inherited as well
as current. They know loss, and they know that everything
that is won can be forfeited again. If it isn't the storm surges
it's time: all this is only borrowed unless you fight for it.
I know the old maps, where I can see with the naked eye
that the border is painfully wrong. As though someone had

pulled a sock much too far up a slightly too thin leg. And
I know that the soil of the borderland has absorbed both
blood and saltwater in a way that's difficult for a person who
grew up on a desolate parish heath north-west of Herning
to fully understand. My childhood region is far from histo-
ry-less. But comparing the Danish–German borderland to
the heaths of central and western Jutland is like comparing
a picture book to Proust's *In Search of Lost Time*: seven
volumes and a madeleine. In this case, rye bread cake: the
Southern Jutish bake sale's version of a sponge.

But back to Rudbøl, because I drove across the border
there yesterday. And I was ready to do a U-turn. I had the old
A–Z on the passenger seat. It has helped me up and down
the coast in a calm, curious fashion. But the thing about
physical maps printed in colour on paper is that they stop
working at borders. On the Danish side of Rudbøl: a clear
and detailed roadmap. On the German side of the border:
empty land, a few isolated place names here and there, but
no indication as to how to get from one place to the next.

'We've got to draw the line somewhere,' they said at the
National Survey and Land Registry. 'This far and no further,' and so moving across the border at Rudbøl was like
driving onto a frozen field where the snow has just fallen.

It wasn't long, either, before I ran into trouble. The man
at the bar had been right. I hit a traffic jam by some road-
works. But before I got too badly stuck, I turned off and
let the GPS lead me down the little roads of North Frisia.
I drove on dikes, down winding routes past proud farms
on old *terps*. The moon rose above the landscape and hung
round and clear in its lapis lazuli sky. Somewhere to the

south-west was Rungholt, with its secrets intact. One day the storm surge will return. People will lie in the darkness and think about the dams. A father's face lit by the phone in the dim bedroom. He can't sleep, what with the news about the water level. Late at night, the evacuation buses are driving back and forth, picking people up. The adults carry sleeping bags, ground pads, children their teddy bears. They have to sleep in the local sports hall. Just until the storm lets up, says their mother. The adults are given soup in coffee mugs. The children get a chocolate biscuit, but then they have to sleep. Tomorrow is another day, and so they lie down among neighbours and strangers. They try to get some rest from the crackling fluorescent light. From the storm that keeps going. They're safe here, but what about the sheep, the cows. And the dog that didn't come with them. And the cat.

'It hid in the roof space,' whispers the child.

'Cats have nine lives,' the mother whispers in the dark, and thinks of the clattering tiles, the salty rain, the future. For the storm surge is coming. But not today, I thought yesterday. Not tomorrow, I think, driving past the border shops in the German town of Aventoft. I didn't go in; I was headed further north. At the pub in Rudbøl, I'd asked the man at the bar whether the crossing at Aventoft was still working as usual.

'Yes,' he said, 'but it's not called that. It's called the Møllehusvej border crossing.'

Understood; and that's how I fall and get back to my feet in the borderland. Setting out across the polders. Driving my path-finding car over dikes, over rural roads. Raising

Quiet Rain in Skagen

A cormorant sat on Grenen, the very northern spit of Denmark. It was winter. It sat alone under its black cloak, turning in the wind, its face stiffened into a grimace of strident will. It turned from one body of water to the other. Looked at the Kattegat, at the Skagerrak, at me. This was just after New Year. I was out alone on Grenen. I wanted to stand there as I'd stood when I was a child, almighty, with a foot in each sea. The wind blew from the south-west. The cold was biting, and out there at Skagen Reef, the seas met like young lovers at a railway station. They ran along the platform, arms out, towards the person they'd been missing. Unable to contain the joy of being reunited, they ended up simply beating into one another. But there sat a cormorant with its determined face. It was resting out there, turning above the land beneath its black wingspan.

I watched it from a safe distance. Thought: Let it have its moment. Grenen will still be here in ten minutes, and in this cold, I can have it to myself once the bird has gone. While I waited, I observed the big cargo ships, the container ships, the coasters. They lay, as always, on the east side of the headland in poetic stasis. Like thousands and thousands of ships before them, they had been lucky getting north around Skagen Reef without going down. They're exhaling, I thought. Or they're steeling themselves to go back over the reef, who knows. They were in smooth waters, in any case. Like rocking caravans during a temporary stay in an oasis. That's what they looked like, but in reality the ships are there, apparently, because they don't know where they're going next. They're awaiting orders from their shipping companies. No point sailing down through inland Danish waters if you're going back to Norway. So they wait. Recover, call home, play cards in their quarters. Or they walk around on deck with binoculars.

'There's a cormorant on Grenen,' a Russian voice might say out there.

'Then we'll wait,' another might respond.

But then the bird flew off, and it was my turn. I approached the place where the two bodies of water met. Kattegat at my right foot. Skagerrak at my left. Year round, every minute of the daylight hours, a person stands at that point, sensing in their own body what it means to be all-powerful. What would it mean to be great? Surely, to be great is to stand at the northernmost tip of the nation, right at the very top, with a foot in each sea. Can you feel the potential? This is your country, your language. Your limitations. In this moment under your jurisdiction, and only yours.

I stood there barefoot as a child. I was afraid of the waves and kept one eye on my mum. Assuming things went the way they usually did, I'd have had to move—first for one big brother, then the second. They'd have wanted to stand there too, and set their feet apart. Be photographed. One brother with chalk-white hair. The other squinting. Their thin arms, sunburnt knees and my feet in the sand, with nail varnish on the big toe. I remembered it the way you remember things you've seen on old photographic slides. On the screen in the living room, my dad in the light of the projector, his seven remaining fingers fumbling with the slides. I can't always tell what memories are mine and what's been told to me, I thought, planting myself in my hiking boots with one foot by each sea. I felt no almighty power. Only cold and tenderness. Surrounded by my country, my language, my limitations.

The plan was to go up Skagen's Grey Lighthouse this winter. I wanted to go up and see the line's beginning with my naked eye. But I had driven all that way to Denmark's northernmost point in vain. The lighthouse had closed for the season. I tugged handles all around the keeper's cabin. I peered in through windows, read signs. Nothing. The lighthouse looked like the barrel of a gun, pointing in hot-tempered defiance at the sky. And open it was definitely not.

I was staying in a rented house in the village of Old Skagen, so I went to the museum instead and took an enjoyable look at the highly Instagrammable lives of painters in the area over the past century. I bought napkins printed with the joys of congregations of artists. Handmade soap. I thought of my mother, walking around Skagen Museum and dreaming of a studio with north-facing windows. One like the artist Anna Ancher's. She walked here dreaming of a life of grapes on pale dishes and Dad's hunting dog at her feet, like Anna's. But in reality, that dog ate our shoes. At some point it learnt to open doors with its paws. One time it mauled Dad's poultry to death, and it wouldn't listen to anyone, not anyone. But my mum dreamt of a life of contemplative beauty under a grand sky, with rose bushes in the garden, on her own terms, and I pottered around in my own dreams: of being like the ladies in the pictures. Yes, when you grow up, you will walk on eternally mild summer beaches. You will sit by the paraffin lamp and write while your lover is preoccupied with his own tasks in the background. You will become a real and beautiful person. You will, but you couldn't, and so you became something else: a movement pinned in one place.

Winter on this line, from north to south, is not for the faint of heart. On the other hand, there is something starkly sober about it, and that was also why I drove to Skagen in January. I wanted to explore the tourist town out of season. I wandered around in the dark down the small gravel roads of Old Skagen. I saw the pretty yellow houses with the traditional white lace on their red roofs. So in there is where they live when the sun is shining, I thought. A single light in a house here and there, but otherwise wet and black, the way I wanted it: Skagen without its summer skirts. Everything except for the harbour and the adjoining local areas and homes reduced to scenery. A tourist town, a holidaymaker's paradise, the metastasizing of the rich in the far-northern wilds of the Danish nation. I walked past the big beachside hotels. On one street: a jacuzzi on the pavement. Put out to wait under a solitary lamp for repair or bulky-waste collection. A rough wind from the south-west. All the cables sticking out of it. God knows what's gone on in there at the height of summer, I thought. Yes, what has it been offered, when the convertibles, the expensive white wine, the bubbles, the cocaine and the royals arrive. Maybe the jacuzzi had seen famous bottoms? It wasn't unlikely. It struck me as lonely and outlived, sitting there under the lamplight. Delivered from its suffering or robbed of its identity.

I found the Sunset Kiosk. I hadn't been since I was little. Every night, people would meet at the kiosk to watch the sun go down. I remembered: we had ice cream. The more orange the sky became, the more people gathered. They drank from wine glasses with long stems, and then came the moment when the sun set in earnest. At the moment the last rind of fire was gone, they clapped. Yes, they clapped the sun in Skagen, and I felt ashamed; I remembered that. To clap the sun was to clap for themselves. Or I sensed that the clapping was ironic, distanced, and that was almost worse. It made the sunset into a piece of theatre, and if the sun was a piece of theatre, then humanity was separate from it: reduced to spectators. One day I would leave my own point of departure, where people never applauded nature. I sensed it as the ice cream's yellow glaze ran down my fingers. What will become of me, I might have thought. But I can never tell what memory is mine and what's been told to me. Including when it comes to the light in Skagen.

It was precisely the light and the raw landscape that attracted the artists and later the tourists to the headland. After his great trip to Jutland in 1859, Hans Christian Andersen praised the authentic, unforgettably windswept northern spit of land, Skagen. He encouraged artists to make a pilgrimage there in their hunt for subject matter.

Presumably this was a kind of reckoning with the ever-green, cosy Biedermeier motifs from Copenhagen and the surrounding areas that he himself had so assiduously cultivated. Andersen was now upgrading the land on the edges. He compared the desert between the two seas with something you'd otherwise have to travel to Africa to see, or Pompeii. After that, they began to drift in and out of the fishing village: the painters, the poets. In 1874, Michael Ancher arrived from Bornholm and settled down. He fell in love with the innkeeper's daughter, the talented Anna. Later came P.S. Krøyer with his assured technique.[1] The poet Holger Drachmann towered among the bright-yellow houses. They wrote poetry, painted, drank and attracted followers. They grew like strange plants up the dunes with their rickety easels. Their subjects: bright, warm, sum-mer-holiday-beautiful. They spent time painting the locals. They spent even more time painting themselves and each other. The infidelity, the alcoholism and the power strug-gles—those they did not paint. They stuck to mouth-blown bottles, dead-calm seas in the moonlight, ruddy-cheeked children and heavy, labia-like velvet curtains. They paved the way for a culture of pilgrimage to Utopia, and what must Anna Ancher, native-born, have thought as they stood there clapping the sun?

Today, the centre of economic power moves to Skagen to eat prawns with mayonnaise a few months out of the year. For the richest people in the country, the motivic reck-oning with the evergreen beech forests never really reached any further south down the coast. Do you know this line because you've been on holiday to Skagen? No, I thought, and this was winter. The Sunset Kiosk was shut. The big beachside hotels were asleep among the dunes like hibernating bears, and I took the car. Drove into Skagen, down to the harbour. I walked, swaddled in my winter coat and big knitted hat, past the enormous trawlers. I enjoyed the pragmatism: the smell of fish, the oil, the petrol and the no-bullshit architecture. The young men walked shivering in joggers and puffer jackets. They were headed for the café, which stays open in winter. Inside, a girl is slinging coffees over the counter. She has a ponytail and a secondary-school certificate. He wants to join her and have the dregs from the percolator. Afterwards, she'll come out for a ride in the car with him. They'll drive around for a bit, and she'll see his new tattoo. She doesn't want to go; or, yeah, she does after all. So he drives her along the route past the Dune House, where the royal family once lived, to the Sand-Covered Church. In the car park near the forest, they sit in darkness, the two of them. He's got to promise her he will do better. She's got to promise she will never move to Aarhus or Copenhagen. Then they put the seats back in the dark, zigzagging down the platform. Arms out, towards the person they've been missing. Unable to contain the joy of being reunited, they end up simply beating into one another.

The year was new. My Toyota crawled down sunken roads, down side streets, along the edges of quays, and it shuddered in the car park in the shelter of the locked public toilets,

'Closed until Easter'. And Easter came, the toilets opened, and I wanted to see the line, beginning or ending up there on the headland. I called the Grey Lighthouse. It was still shut. They were preparing to reopen late. I said I couldn't wait. My year was running out.

'Just come up here, and I'll let you in,' said the caretaker, and so I drove.

I drove north from the place where I live, up along the coast. I followed the line across the channel at Thyborøn, up across Thy through the wildlife reserves. I swung the car from Vigsø Bay to Misery Bay, up through Vendsyssel to Hirtshals. Along the way, I stopped to find amber-yellow oyster shells on the beach between Uggerby and Tversted, but then pushed onwards, further north, along Tannis Bay to Skagen in the swelling spring. I checked into a hotel close to the supermarket, unpacked and put my notebook in my bag. Then I set off for Grenen. I had my sights on the last lighthouse on the route. I parked the car between the keeper's cabin and a funny little square black shed. It was so unassuming that I hadn't seen it in winter, even though it had satellite dishes and antennae on the roof. There were 'No Entry' signs in several languages on the road that led up to it. Outside was a shiny blue car, but there was no glimpse of anyone through the windows.

There was, however, a man in the keeper's cabin. He was waiting for me among stuffed birds. The keeper's cabin is a centre for migrating birds. Coffee pots stood in line on the counter in front of him, ready for a new season.

'I can't offer you coffee,' he said. 'Technically we're closed.'

'That's okay,' I replied. 'I don't want to put you out.'

But I wasn't putting him out, I could tell, so I asked if he knew anything about the black shed north of the light-house car park.

'Ah, well, there's a man in there,' said the caretaker. 'He's been there since the Cold War. Well, they probably send a new one every once in a while, but there's always a man in there. At one point he kept an eye on Soviet submarines. Now probably just whatever's going on over Skagen Reef. They're among the busiest waters in the world.'

We went over to the cabin window and peered out together at the shed. There it was on its dune, not far from my car.

'So the Ministry of Defence sends a single man up here to keep an eye on national security from that thing?' I asked, pointing at the black shed.

'Yup. At one time there were two of them, apparently,' said the caretaker, 'but then the Berlin Wall fell.'

The caretaker had a warm smile.

'It's very Danish,' I said, 'setting up something that looks like a camper van and sending a man with binoculars to guard some of the busiest waters in the world.'

'Not sure about binoculars,' said the caretaker, 'but every now and then he goes out for a smoke.'

'Don't tell that to Putin,' I said.

Then we smiled, and the caretaker showed me around his bird museum. There were golden eagles in the loft above him, pink-footed geese and a single wood pigeon. At one point, the East Atlantic migration route was visualized as a glowing line through the world, and as we walked, touching panels and plastered walls, I told him I had once lived in

Copenhagen but now lived by the sea, only further down. And he told me he had once been a postman over there. Meaning in Copenhagen. 'But the city does something to time,' he said. 'It's all so laborious. Here you're never more than ten minutes from anywhere.' Where I live it's a bit more, but otherwise it's the same, and then we talked about the schism, the caretaker and I. The one in which all identity is formed, and which one must renounce or learn to live with at some point, when you're born into a culture where you don't applaud the sun.

'I move a lot,' I said.

'And I get the benefit of Copenhagen coming here three months out of the year,' he said. 'The rest of the time it's pretty peaceful.'

By now we'd reached the stairs, and he pointed up the tower.

'You'd best go by yourself,' he said, so I did, and now here I am.

It's started drizzling, and the Grey Lighthouse is already damp. Pointing the barrel of its gun indefinitely towards the light, which is supposed to be so special in Skagen. Behind me, I have the dream of eternal summer, and from the harbour everything sets sail. I love the raw and practical lure of the foreign in this line, and before me the headland stretches its sandy tentacle across the water, becoming a branch in the rain. Such quiet spring rain in Skagen. It makes everything scented. I can smell the salt, the seaweed, the crowberry stalks. Steam rises from the line, and there it is, the cormorant, in the cold of winter. Its wilful face, its glossy feathered cloak. I shut my eyes in the Grey

Lighthouse. I take my time; there's nothing else I have to do. It's Saturday night. My dad is fumbling in the light of the projector for the next slide, and then the next. My mum has baked cream puffs. The device smells metallic. It sounds like a dull knife being sharpened every time a new image is pushed in front of the light. There's my brother with his white hair. There are the squinting eyes. The seas meet. A ship sails across the reef, and there's the girl. Her hand is sticky with ice cream. She's standing on a coastline with a foot in each sea. She will stay, she will go, she can do nothing else.

LIST OF PLACES

'The Line': Vedersø Dune, Vedersø.

'The Shortest Night': Skallerup Dune, Tornby Dune Forest, Hirtshals and Rubjerg Knude.

'Wandering Houses': Børglum Abbey, Rubjerg Knude, Mårup, Lønstrup, Løkken, Holmsland Dune, Lyngvig, Lyngvig Lighthouse Lønborg Heath, Ringkøbing Fjord.

'The Secret Place': Harboøre, Thyborøn, Nissum Broad, Langerhuse, Harboøre Peninsula, Thy, Rønland.

'West by Water': Blåvandshuk, Horns Mount, Horns Reef, Skallingen, Kallesmærsk Heath, Oksbøl, Varde, Mosevrå, Esbjerg, Ribe.

'The Tracks around Bulbjerg': Bulbjerg, Skarre Cliff, Ringkøbing Fjord, Oddesund.

'The Timeless': Old Parish Church, Staby Church, Dybe Church, Bovbjerg, Ferring Church on the stretch of coast between Ringkøbing Fjord and the Limfjord, Bøvling Dune, Nissum Fjord, Thorsminde.

'Amsterdam, Hvide Sande': Amsterdam and Hvide Sande, Skjern River, Ringkøbing Fjord, Holmsland Dune.

'Wadden Sea Suite': Huisduinen, Den Helder, Texel, Holland / Sønderho, Fanø, Esbjerg, the West, East and North Frisian islands, Ribe.

'"In My Distress"': Groningen, Vejers, Henne, Vedersø Dune / Vedersø, Thorsminde, Harboøre, Fjand, Blåvandshuk.

'Winter Solstice': Thy, Thyborøn Channel, Agger Peninsula, Agger, Lodbjerg Lighthouse, Lodbjerg Church, Hjardemål Church, Hanstholm, Klitmøller, Tranum Dune Forest, Jammerbugten, Vigsø Bay.

'Magnets': Wadden Sea, Skallingen, Mandø, Rømø, Fanø, Vester Vedsted, Ribe, Havneby, List.

'Borderland': Sylt, Listland, Rudbøl, Fanø, Rømø, Dagebüll, Keitum, Rungholt, Ejdum, Nordstrand, the marshland locks, Kongeå River, Margrethe Polder, New Frederik's Polder, Old Frederik's Polder, Rødding, North Frisia, Aventoft.

'Quiet Rain in Skagen': Skagen, Old Skagen, Vigsø Bay, Jammerbugten, Vendsyssel, Hirtshals, Uggerby, Tversted, Tannis Bay.

REFERENCES

The Line

1 Kerstin Ekman, *En by af lys* ('A City of Light'),
   Gyldendal 1983.

Wandering Houses

1 Gert Jensen, *Børglum Kloster—fra kongsgård til
   herregård* ('Børglum Abbey: From Royal Estate to
   Manor House'), Forlaget Vendsyssel 2006.
2 Knud Sørensen, *Kun slutningen mangler* ('Only the End
   is Missing'), Gyldendal 2008, p. 30.
3 *Ibid.*, p. 33.

The Secret Place

1 Steen Ulnits, 'Cheminova—en tikkende giftbombe'
   ('Cheminova: A Ticking Poison Bomb'), www.Ulnits.
   dk/biologi/cheminova-timeline, 2018.

2 'Er det bedst bare at glemme de 110 tons gift, der ligger begravet på stranden?' ('Is It Best to Just Forget the 110 Tons of Poison Buried on the Beach?'), www.zetland.dk/historie/s81E7jBK-ae7E79wm-23540, 12 December 2019.

West by Water

1 *Bunker-Mule* (1995), Blåvand-Oksby, made by the British artist Bill Woodrow.
2 Jeanette Varberg, *Viking—Ran, ild og sværd* ('Viking: Plunder, Fire and Sword'), Gyldendal 2019, p. 286.
3 *Ibid.*, p. 241.
4 Michael Pye, *The Edge of the World: How the North Sea Made Us Who We Are*, Penguin Books 2015, p. 70.

The Tracks around Bulbjerg

1 Kerstin Ekman, *Hændelser ved vand* ('Events by Water'), trans. Anne Marie Bjerg, Samlerens Forlag 1993, p. 429.
2 *Ibid.*, p. 282.

The Timeless

1 Knud Sørensen, 'Det ottekantede forsamlingshus' ('The Octagonal Town Hall') in *Jul på Mors—Lokalhistorisk Årsskrift*, Museum Mors 2016.
2 Psalm 36:5.
3 Benedicte Ostersen, 'Danske kalkmalerier overlevede reformationen' ('Danish Frescoes Survived the

Reformation'), an interview with the art historian Hans Jørgen Frederiksen, www.kristendom. dk/danmark/danske-kalkmalerier-overlevede-reformationen, 19 February 2013.

4 Varberg, *op. cit.*, p. 402.

5 The oldest fresco in Dybe Church was painted in 1525 by Esger Andersen, also called the Master of Lemvig.

Wadden Sea Suite

1 Steffen M. Søndergaard, *Gamle huse i Sønderho* ('The Old Houses of Sønderho'), Fanø Kommune, Fredningsstyrelsen 1980.

2 Ina Kjøgx Pedersen, *Samles, skilles ad: Erindringer om liv og død i Sønderho* ('Gather, Scatter: Memories of Life and Death in Sønderho'), Gyldendal 2010.

'In My Distress'

1 Gert Normann Andersen, *Skibsvragenes kyst— Dramatiske strandinger fra Thyborøn til Vedersø Klit* ('Shipwreck Coast: Dramatic Wrecks from Thyborøn to Vedersø Dune'), Sea War Museum Jutland 2017.

2 Inger Bjørn Knudsen (ed.), Christian Ringskou et al., *Jernkysten*, Lemvig Museum 2017, and www. jernkysten.dk.

3 Palle Uhd Jepsen, *Den sidste rejse—Historien om linjeskibene HMS* St. George *og HMS* Defence *og deres tid til de forliste på Jyllands vestkyst d. 24. december 1811* ('The Last Voyage: The Story of the Ships of the

Line HMS *St George* and HMS *Defence* and Their Era until Their Sinking on the West Coast of Jutland on 24 December 1811'), De Kulturhistoriske Museer in Holstebro Kommune 2017, pp. 162–5.

4 The St George Shipwreck Museum was designed by architects Frank Maali and Gemma Lalanda.

Winter Solstice

1 Isaiah 40:9.

2 Mogens Møller, 'Bent Jernstang og besætterne' ('Bent Jernstang and the Occupiers'), www.nordjyske.dk/nyheder/bent-jernstang-og-besaetterne/1b59d2f1-09bf-499d-89ac-e2a72fd8d7bb, 7 May 2008.

3 Tove Ditlevsen: 'Min karriere' in *Jeg ville være enke, og jeg ville være digter—Glemte tekster*, Gyldendal 2015, p. 32.

4 Bjarne S. Bendtsen, review of *Hanstholm. Drømmen om en havn* ('Hanstholm: A Dream of a Port') by Knud Holch Andersen, Flemming Skipper and Jens Andersen, www.historie-online.dk/boger/anmeldelser-5-5/lokal-og-slaegtshistorie/ hanstholm-droemmen-om-en-havn, undated.

Magnets

1 Everything I know about wetland birds and the East Atlantic migration route I learnt at the outstanding Vadehavscentret or Wadden Sea Centre. My thanks to the centre and its director, Klaus Melbye.

2 The Wadden Sea Centre was designed by the architect Dorte Mandrup, and was awarded the 2017 prize for Building of the Year in Denmark.

Borderland

1 Irene Petersen, 'Sandkorn vidner om katastrofal superstorm i Danmark' ('Grains of Sand Testify to a Catastrophic Superstorm in Denmark'), videnskab. dk/kultur-samfund/sandkorn-vidner-om-katastrofal-superstorm-i-danmark, 4 March 2013.
2 Michael Pye, *op. cit.*, p. 44.

Quiet Rain in Skagen

1 Neil Kent, *The Triumph of Light and Nature: Nordic Art 1740–1940*, Thames & Hudson 1992, p. 105.

AUTHOR'S
ACKNOWLEDGEMENTS

A book like this does not write itself, and I have met many incredibly helpful people along the way. Most of you, those who gave me directions and told me things, I don't know by name. You stood in lighthouses, in cafés, in museum shops, in grocery stores. You're out there, this is your landscape, and I will not forget you. Thank you, Signe Parkins, for the beautiful drawings and for escorting me on a fresco-search for the timeless. Thanks to my Danish editor Julie Paludan-Müller, and a big thank you to Adam Freudenheim and Kirsten Chapman at Pushkin Press and Fiona McCrae and Yuka Igarashi at Graywolf Press. Also: thank you to Brigid Hughes, *A Public Space*, New York, who believed in me in the first place. Thanks to Helle Henningsen, Ellen Deckwitz, Victor Nielsen, Ylva Østby, Jens Böhme, Ove and Susanne Pedersen, Frida Thornvig, Camilla Stockmarr, Kamilla Hega Holst, Mads Nygaard, Knud Sørensen, and Birthe J (you know who you are). You have guided me, lent me books, looked after the house, looked after the cat, given me directions, unlocked doors, and some of you have even joined me on my journey. Thanks also to Edith Södergran, Tom Kristensen, Kerstin Ekman and an old folksong from Fanø, because I was allowed to talk to them along the way. Special thanks to Anne Mette Lundtofte and Søren Lind for ongoing conversations about everything and anything to do with writing, life and the world. Thanks to Realdania! Thanks to the Dutch Foundation for Literature for the opportunity to live and work at your retreat in the water-controllers' paradise of Amsterdam. It was unforgettable, so 'dank je wel'. For another couple of stays at the Danish Centre for Writers and Translators, Hald Hovedgaard: thank you; and a huge thanks to my translator Caroline Waight. Same goes for Ahlander Agency in Stockholm. You rock. To those with whom I share my fascination with the wild and gentle landscape: Benny, Vibeke, Victor, Sofie and Mikael, as well as my parents, Ruth and Egon, who handed down their love for western Denmark and a well-thumbed A–Z: neither my little Toyota nor I would have found our way without you.

DORTHE NORS

Vedersø, October 2021

Dorthe Nors is the author of the story collections *Wild Swims* and *Karate Chop*; four novels, including *Mirror, Shoulder, Signal*, a finalist for the Man Booker International Prize; and two novellas, collected in *So Much for That Winter*. Her short stories have appeared in numerous international publications, including the *New Yorker, Boston Review*, and *Harper's*. She lives on the North Sea coast of Denmark.

Caroline Waight is a literary translator working from Danish, German, and Norwegian. She has translated a wide range of fiction and nonfiction, with recent publications including *The Lobster's Shell* by Caroline Albertine Minor, *Island* by Siri Ranva Hjelm Jacobsen, and *The Chief Witness* by Sayragul Sauytbay and Alexandra Cavelius. She lives and works near London.